Creative Christmas Carvings

By Tina Toney

FOX BOOKS
Fox Chapel Publishing Co Inc.

Publisher:	Alan Giagnocavo
Project Editor:	Ayleen Stellhorn
Desktop Specialist:	Linda L. Eberly, Eberly Designs Inc.
Interior Photography:	Marvin Pierson, B.P. S.
Cover Photography:	Carl Shuman, Owl Hill Studios

ISBN # 1–56523–120–1

To order your copy of this book,
please send check or money order
for $14.95 plus $2.50 shipping to:
Fox Books
1970 Broad Street
East Petersburg, PA 17520

Manufactured in Korea

Table Of Contents

INTRODUCTION

This book contains patterns and instructions for making 24 ornaments carved from turnings or basswood lumber. The turnings are available commercially. You can also refer to the patterns and make your own turnings from basswood using your own lathe. The flat ornaments are cut from 3/8"-thick basswood.

Many times at shows or during carving classes, carvers tell me they have a difficult time finding the products that I use to paint and finish my carvings. You'll find a list of colors that I commonly use in this book on pages 1 and 2.

Remember, put safety first and practice safe carving skills. Use a glove to protect the hand that holds the carving. Keep your tools sharp! Enjoy!—*Tina Toney*

Sources For Basswood Turnings
Beaver Dam Decoys
3311 Warren-Meadville Road.
State Route 305
PO BOX 40
Cortland OHIO 44410
(330) 637-4007

GETTING STARTED WITH TURNINGS & CUT-OUTS

The three-dimensional ornaments in this book are carved from commercially bought basswood turnings. You can also use the patterns to make your own turnings on a lathe. The relief-carved ornaments are cut from 3/8"-thick basswood.

Tools and Sharpening

To make the projects in this book, you'll need a set of miniature palm chisels, a set of standards, plus a #11, 1/8" u-gouge and a #3, 1/2" sweep. In addition to these, you'll also need a carving knife, a hobby knife with a Testor's Blade®, a leather strop, a good quality carving glove and a non-slip mat for your work surface. Vet Wrap® is another useful item. It is available at feed stores and is commonly used for wrapping animals' legs. I use it like a thumb guard, as shown on page 4. Vet Wrap is also available in flesh color at any pharmacy in the first aid section, although for a much higher cost.

Sharpening is an important skill, but one I can not teach you in this book. There are many great books available on how to sharpen, but nothing replaces being shown the techniques.

I have been sharpening my own tools since I began carving. I have used water stones, oil stones, diamond stones, wet water wheels... you name it, I have it! Once I learned to sharpen, I found that all of these items worked well. I currently use the Razor-Sharp Edgemaking System® to quickly take care of most of the sharpening required during my carving classes. It requires a double-shaft motor, which turns at about 3200 rpm.

Patterns

Before you draw the patterns onto the projects carved on the turnings, locate the center and quarter lines. Locate the arch of the growth rings on the turning. Draw a line dissecting the turning in half in the center of the growth ring arch. Continue up and over the turning, down and across the bottom with the line until it is divided into half. Locate a second line across the bottom of the turning at 90 degrees to the centerline. Proceed up the turning on both sides until it is quartered. Locate the center of the face on a halved side with the arch of the growth rings.

Using the pictures as a guide, draw the pattern lines onto the turnings. You can try to use graphite paper to trace the patterns onto the turning, but I must warn you that it's nearly impossible to accomplish on a round turning. To make it easier, trace a small segment of the design, such as the face, then transfer that portion. Then trace another small segment, such as the arms and the shoulder areas. Keep going in this manner until you have transferred the majority of the pattern onto the turning.

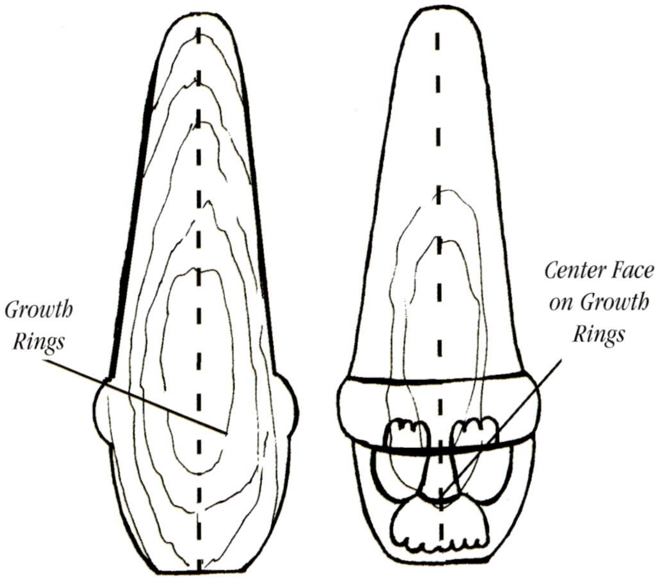

Before you begin carving, look the piece over very closely to check for balance. Are the arms the same size? Are the shoulders located at the same height? Is the belt the same width in front as in the back? Are the feet the same size? If anything does not match, correct it now, before you take knife in hand.

Painting

All the carving projects in this book are painted with acrylic craft colors and mediums. These products are odorless and non-toxic. I use Deco Art™ Americana colors. I find their colors to be lively and cover easily without added layers. Some colors are more transparent and Deco Art indicates this on the labels. Each color has its own product number and is very easy to locate in your favorite craft store.

Drying time for acrylic paints varies according to the humidity and the weather. The mediums you choose will help you to control the paints for a longer period of time and aid in their application.

On very low humidity days, acrylic paint, without an additive, will dry too quickly. This will cause the project to appear plastic-like as subsequent layers are applied. If you plan to paint your project on a low humidity day, add a few drops of medium to your fresh water receptacle. I use Easy Float®.

On very high humidity days, the acrylic paint nearly refuses to dry. To help, use a hair dryer set on low and hold it away from the carving. Holding the dryer too close to your painted piece can cause the paint to dry too quickly, producing blisters.

The eye detail on some ornaments are embellished with a permanent ink pen. Many permanent pens are available in different sizes and colors. I used a Pigma .005 permanent black pen for the projects in this book. A quick misting of Deco Art® Matte DAS13 sets and protects the inked areas prior to the application of final varnish.

As for painting techniques, you'll find a step-by-step demonstration starting on page 14. All of the projects in this book were painted using these techniques, with the exception of the Apple Santa on page 53. That piece was painted using washes of colors overall.

Here is a list of Deco Art Americana colors that are used on the pieces in this book:

FACES: Medium Flesh DA102 over the face. Shading Flesh DA137 floated around the face at the edges and adjacent to the nose. DeLanes Cheek Color DA182 for color on the cheeks. Washes of any red for extra color.

EYES: Williamsburg Blue DA40 or Burnt Sienna DA63 with Lamp Black DA67 pupil and Snow White DA01 highlight.

HAIR, EYEBROWS AND BEARDS: Light Buttermilk DA 164

FUR TRIM ON CLOTHING: Buttermilk DA03

SANTA'S CLOTHING: The Project Santa's (page 3) and Grandfather Frost's (page 23) clothes are Navy Blue DA 35 shaded with Lamp Black DA 67 and drybrushed with Sky Blue Pearl DA 121. The Santa in Blue Jean's (page 19) pants are Uniform Blue DA86 and Lamp Black. The Icicle Santa (page 27) was painted with Burgundy Wine DA22 shaded with Lamp Black. The Bell Santa's (page 33) hat is Black Green DA 157 with Liquitex Opal Green drybrushed over the Black Green. True Red DA129, Napthol Red DA104, Santa Red DA170 and Country Red DA18 are used on the remainder of the Santa's.

SNOWMEN: The basecoat is Uniform Blue DA86, stippled over with Snow White DA01 or Light Buttermilk DA164. The tree on top of the Snowman is painted with Black Green DA157, Kelly Green DA55 and colors of your choice for dots on the tree. The hat is painted Black Green with Green Pearl DA122 stippled over. His scarf is Country Red DA18 with Snow White dots. The noses on the Snowmen are Tangelo orange DA196 with a highlight of Tangelo Orange and Snow White. Lamp Black DA67 is used for the eyes and the buttons.

THE BUSINESSMAN: The coat and hat are painted Lamp Black. The hat band and pants are Graphite DA161. A lighter stripe for the pants is mixed using the Graphite and Snow White.

CHEF BURGERFRIER: Eyes are Burnt Sienna DA63. The hat and coat are Snow White.

Sealer

Upon completion of the painting, it's always a good idea to seal your work, especially should you decide to antique the carvings. I like to seal my carvings with a light misting of Americana Acrylic Sealer/Finisher DAS13 Matte Spray to set the ink if I have used a permanent pen to embellish the top eyelids or other parts of the carving. I then seal the carving overall with Deco Art Matte Varnish DS14. This product is applied with a brush. No further steps need to be taken if you are not going to antique the carving.

Antiquing

Only eight of the ornaments in this book have been antiqued using Trewax Floor Paste Wax in Indian Sand and Clear. They are: Icicle Santa, Chubby Cheeks, Père Noël, Niklaus, Primitive Santa, Baldy Santa, Chubby Santa and the Santa with the Tipped Hat.

Antiquing is a simple procedure. Using a soft lint-free cloth and an old soft toothbrush, I apply the wax to the areas I want to antique. For any ornament that has red clothing, apply the Indian Sand wax overall. For a carving that has an incompatible color of clothing, such as blue or green, apply the Indian Sand wax only to the fur trim, beard, hair and face. The Indian Sand would not enhance the blue of the project piece, yet it would be a nice touch on the fur, hair and face.

Once the colored wax has been applied, immediately follow with an application of the Clear wax to pull off any excess colored wax. You may work back and forth on these small carvings until you are satisfied with the color. Allow the wax to dry about three minutes before buffing it with a soft cloth. Never let the wax dry over 5 minutes. If the wax dries completely, it is very hard to remove from cracks and crevices. Apply a second quick application of the Clear wax, then buff, adding another layer of protection. Buff the piece occasionally with a soft cloth, and it will be years before another application is necessary.

Woodburning

A woodburner is certainly not required to finish a wood carving, but I happen to own one and like the effect it creates. I did not use the woodburner on the main project for this book. There are other carvings that have obviously been woodburned. The use of a woodburner, however, is totally optional.

Power Carving

If you are into power carving, go for it. I like to use power on occasion myself, but again it is totally optional, and I do not address it in this book.

CARVING THE PROJECT SANTA

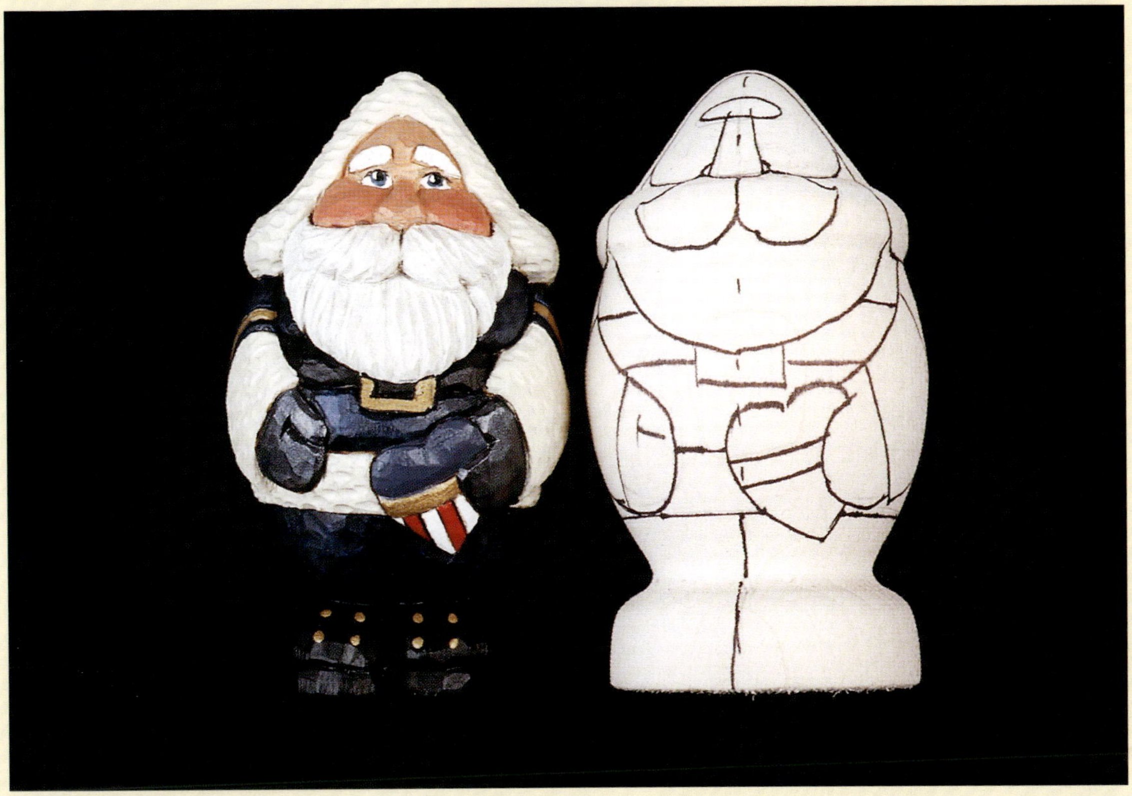

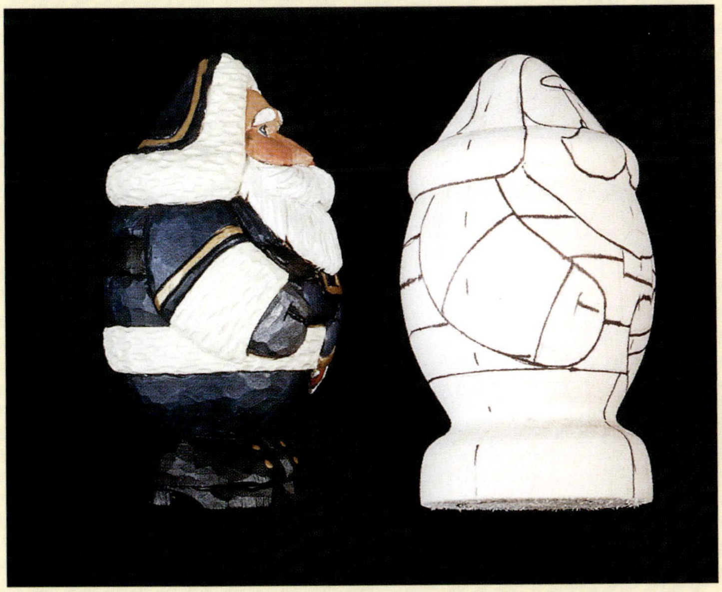

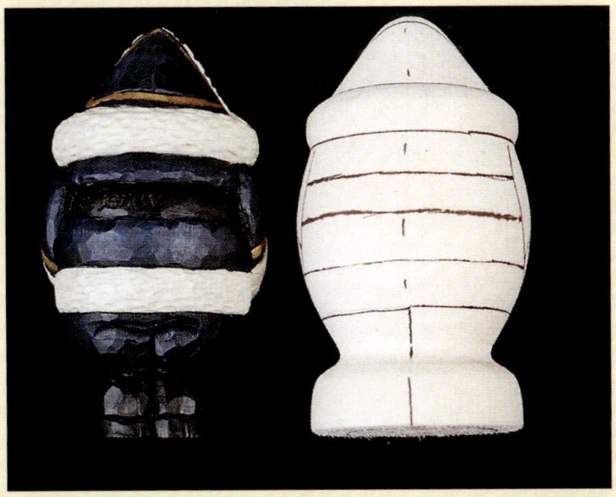

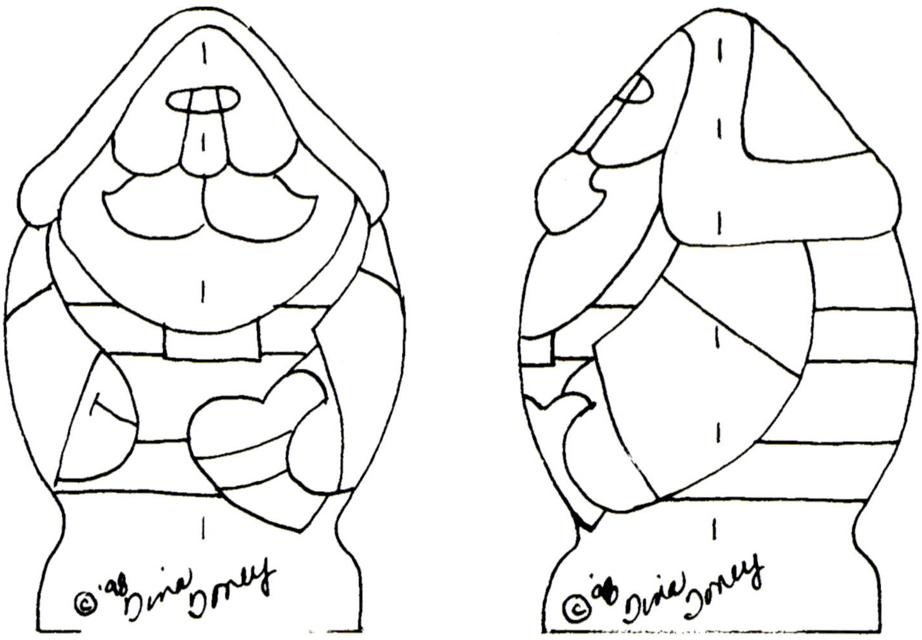

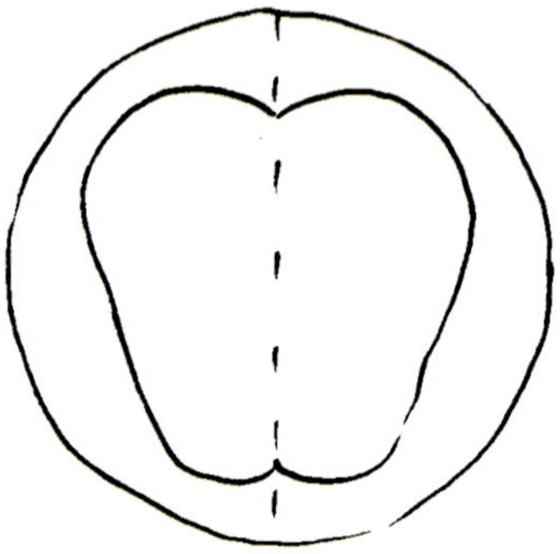

Note: The Project Santa is carved on Footed Egg Shape #TT–02.

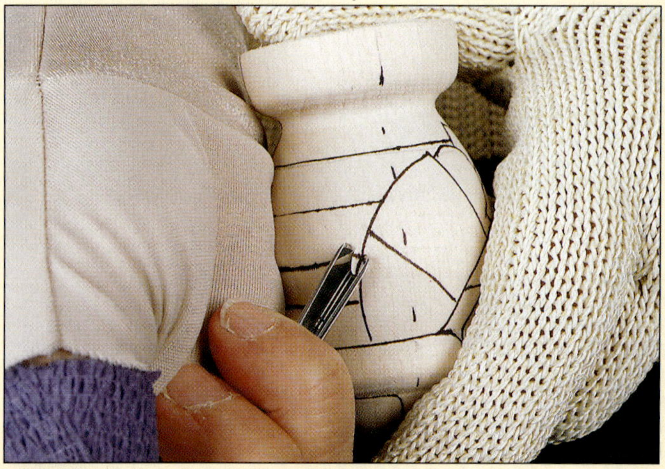

1 Using a v-tool, stop cut behind the arm.

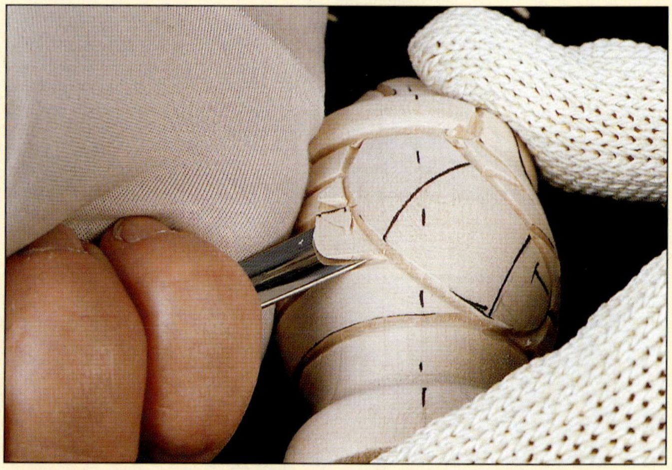

2 A sweep is used to remove wood behind the arms.

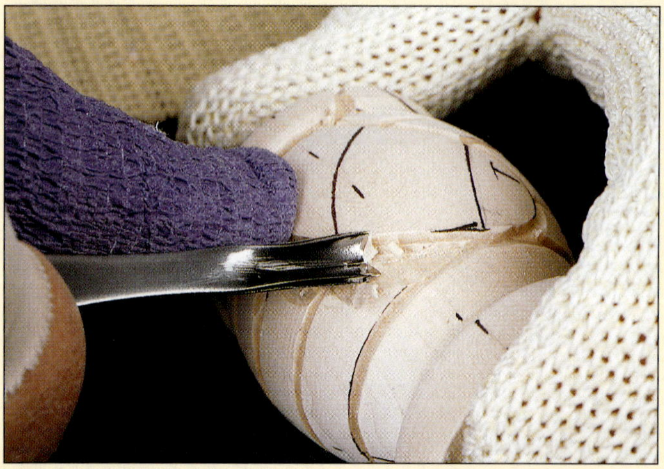

3 Use the v-tool again to deepen and clean the back of the arms.

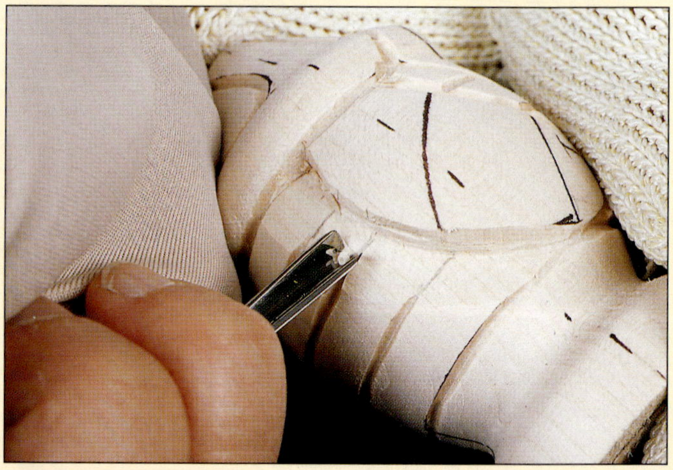

4 A v-tool is used here to stop cut the belt lines.

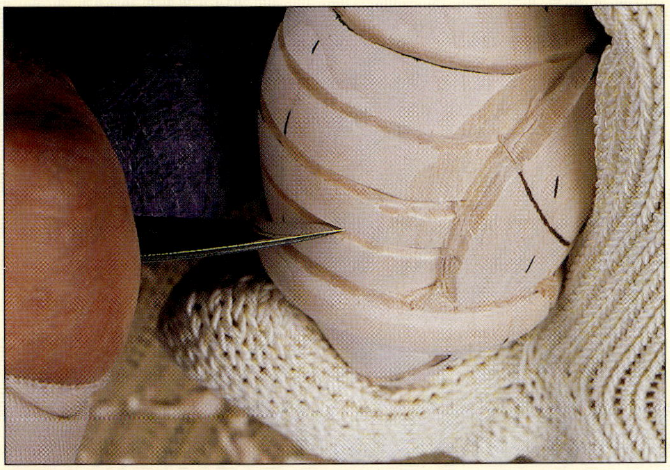

5 *A knife can be used to deepen the stop cut for the belt.*

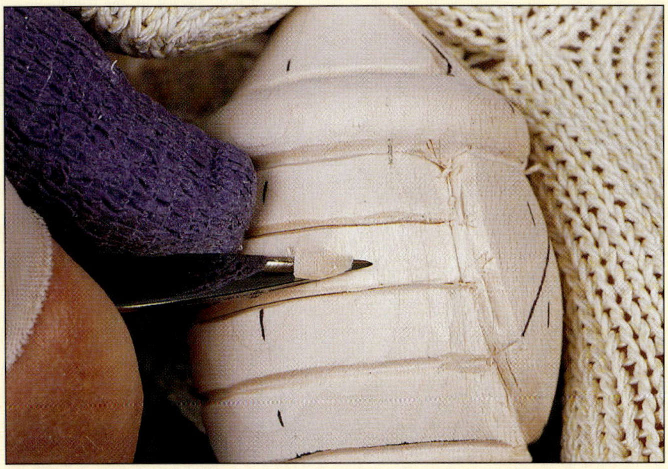

6 *Remove the wood from the belt to help create a cinched-in appearance.*

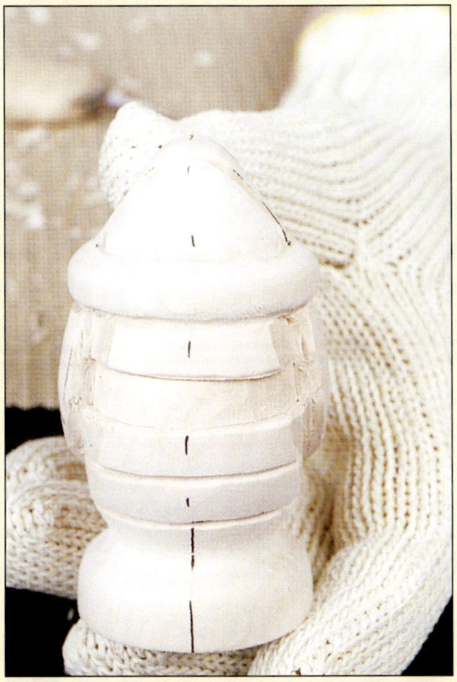

7 *Check to see that an equal amount of wood has been removed behind both arms.*

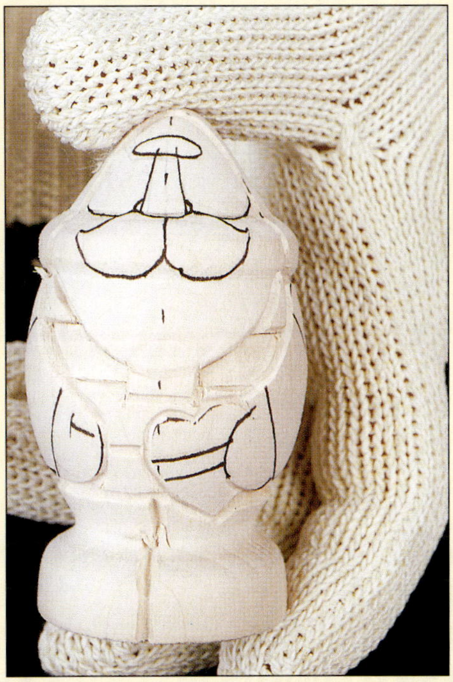

8 *This photo shows the Santa from the front with the major stop cuts set in with a v-tool and the wood around the belt removed.*

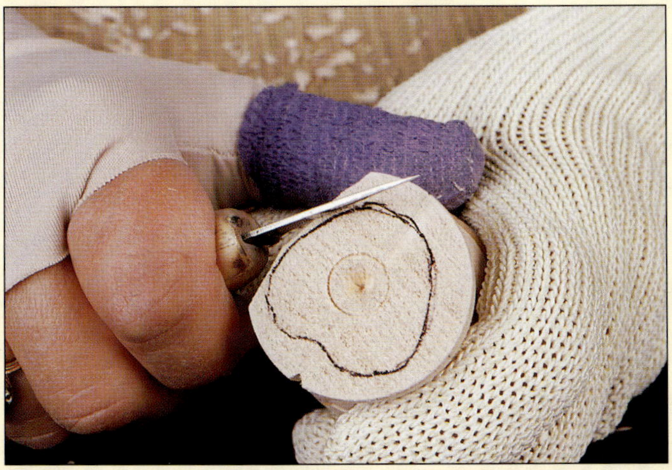

9 *Use a knife to remove excess wood around the boots.*

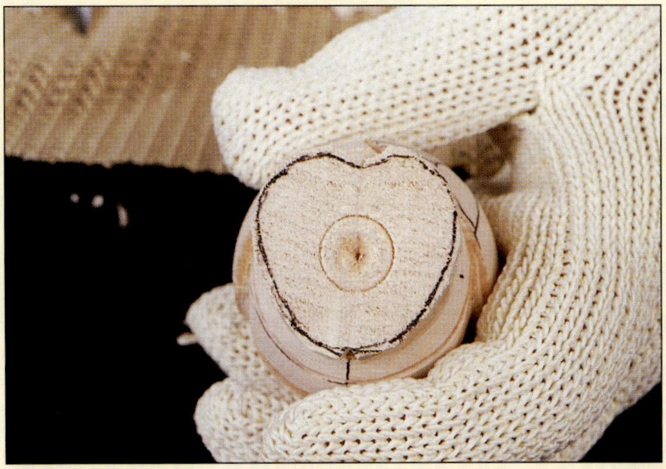

10 *The boots are now roughed in.*

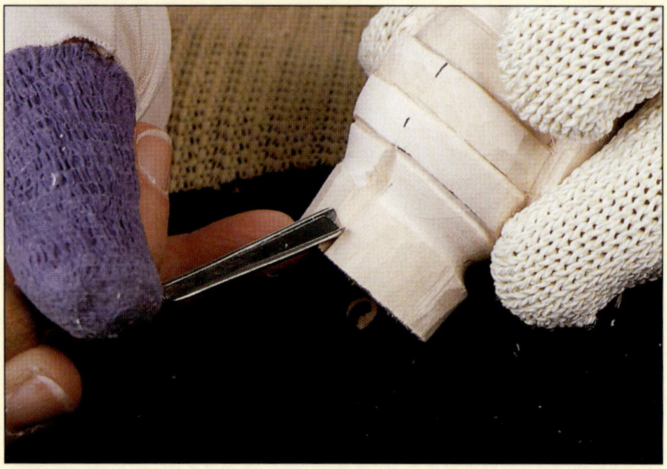

11 *Use a v-tool to separate the back of the boots and the trousers.*

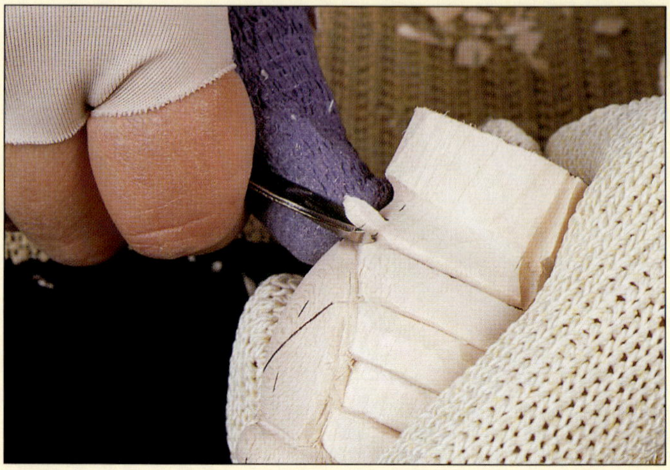

12 *Lay the v-tool on its side and remove the wood below the fur trim on the coat. This allows the trousers to recede underneath the coat. By using the v-tool in this manner, the apex lays against the stop cut to guide the chisel. At the same time, the chisel is used as a straight chisel.*

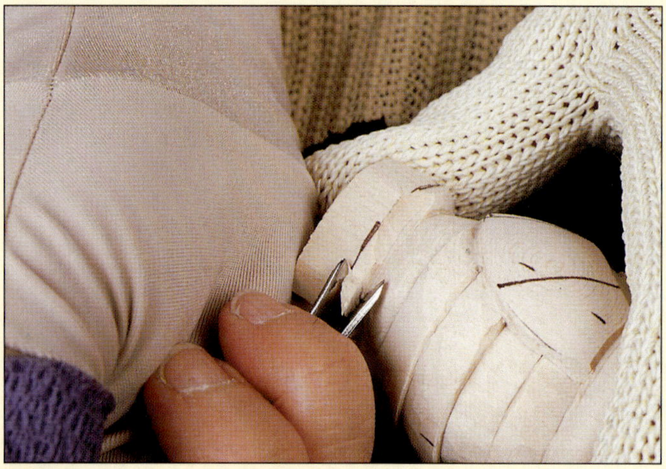

13 *V-tool around the turning to separate the boots from the pants*

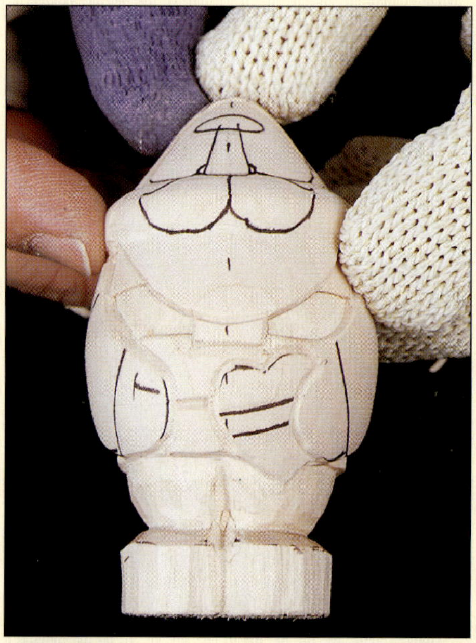

14 *Carve off the sanded surface of the pants.*

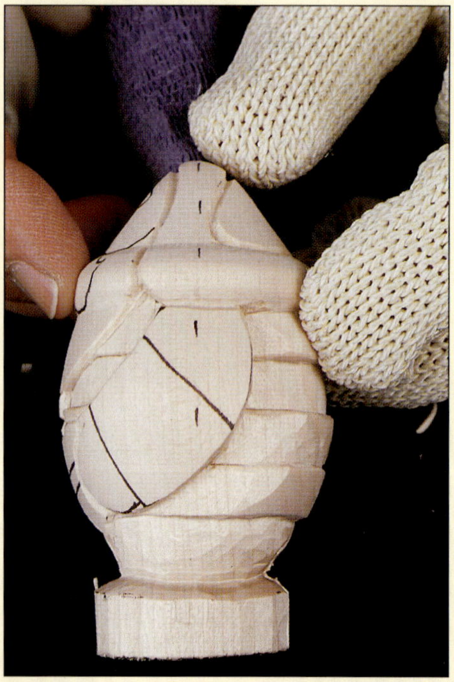

15 *Checking the left profile...*

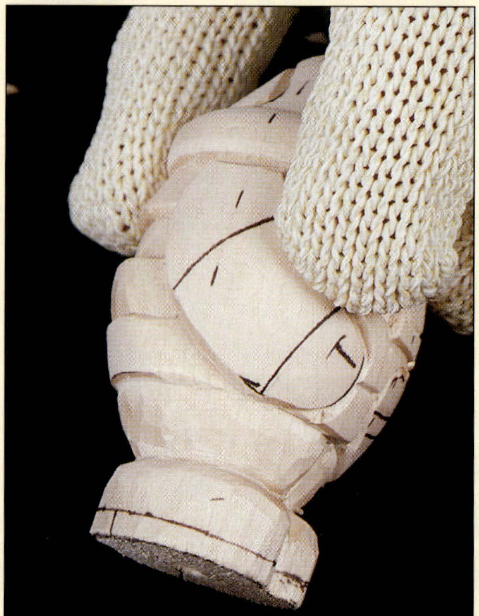

16 *This right profile shows the boot heels and soles drawn.*

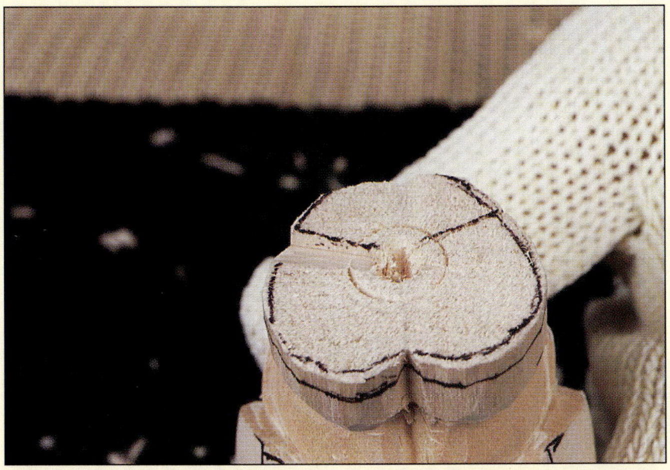

17 *On the bottoms of boots, make a stop cut on the heel line and remove a small wedge.*

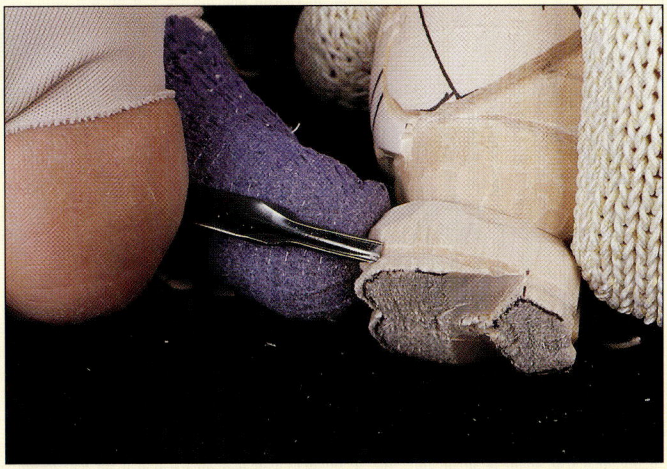

18 *V-tool around the sole of the boot.*

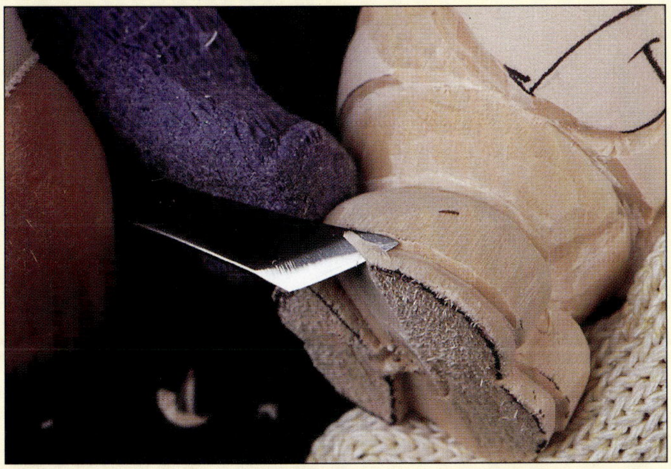

19 *Use a skew to remove the flare.*

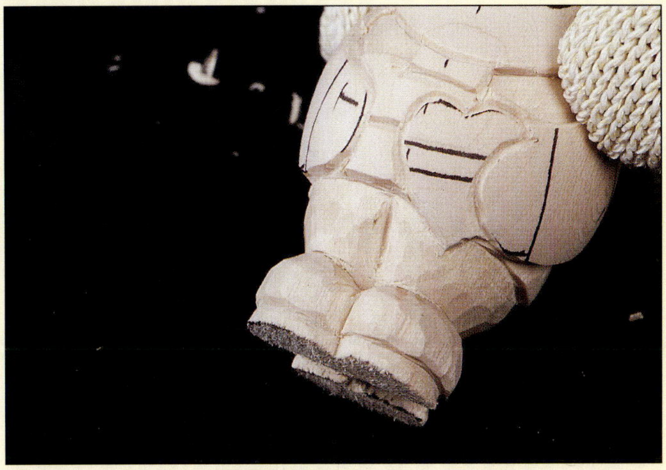

20 *This is what the boot should look like at this point.*

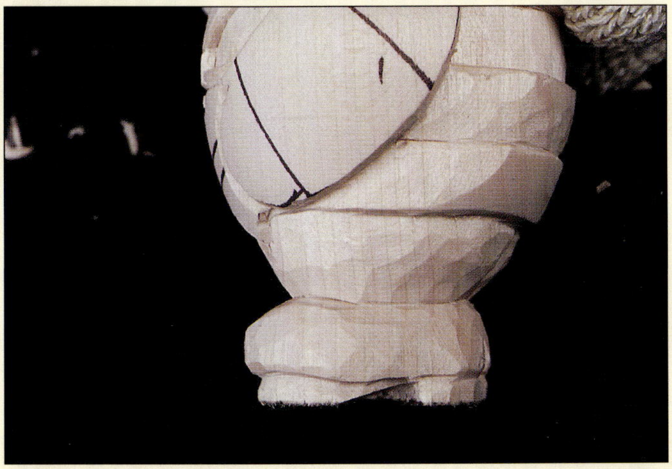

21 *Checking the boot from the side...*

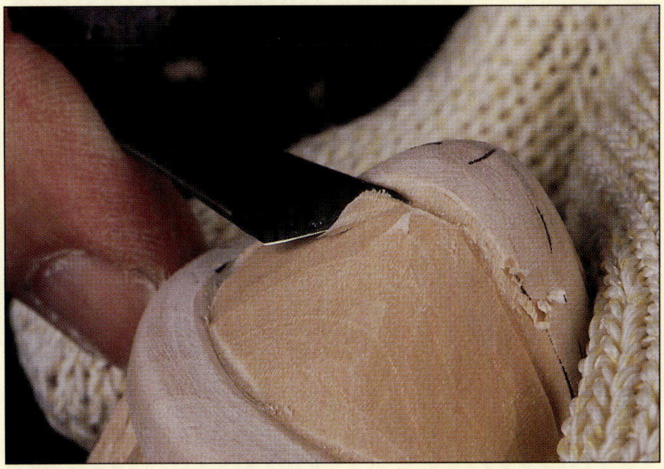

22 *Stop cut around the hat and use a skew to remove the sanded surface.*

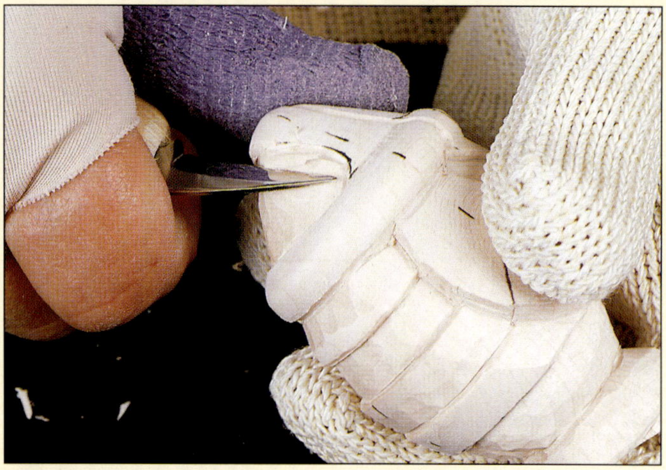

23 *A knife can do the same job as a skew.*

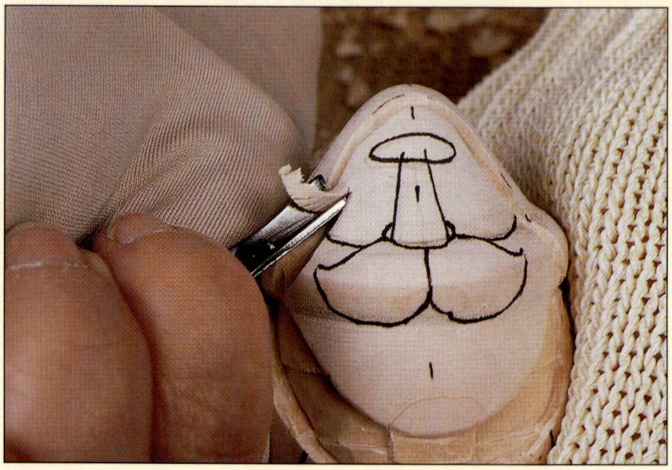

24 *The larger U-gouge from a standard set narrows the face.*

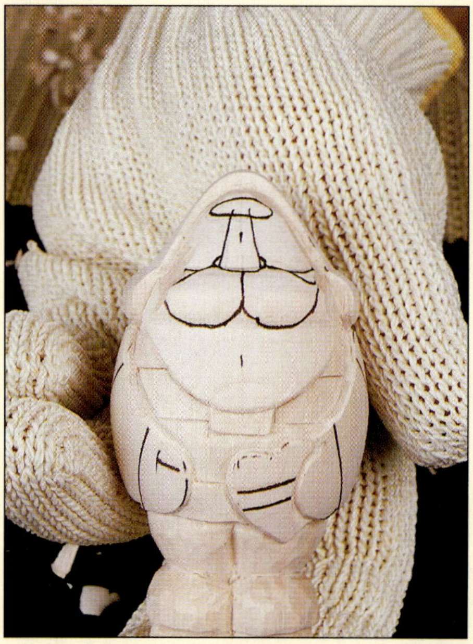

25 *Check that both sides are equal, then carve the pants.*

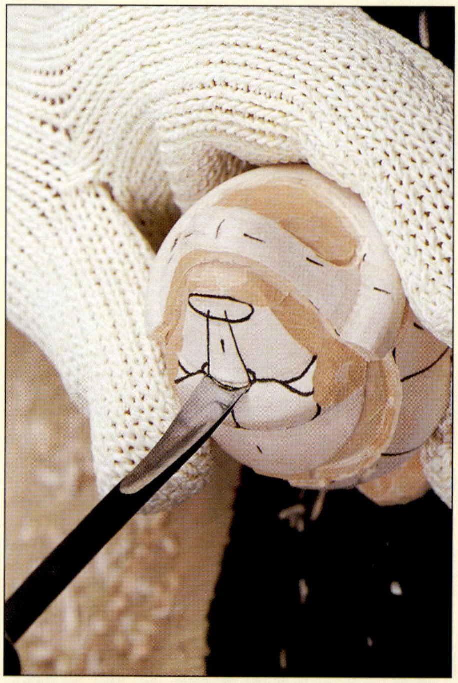

26 *The same U-gouge sets the bottom of the nose. Remember, you may rock the gouge back and forth, but never twist it, as the corners may break.*

27 *Make a stop cut and remove a small wedge of wood beneath nose.*

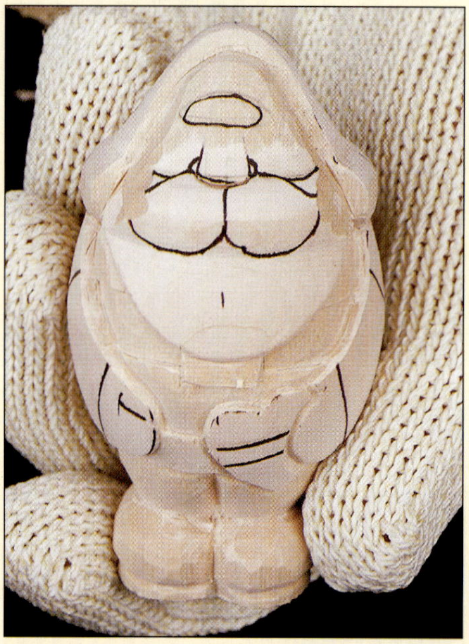

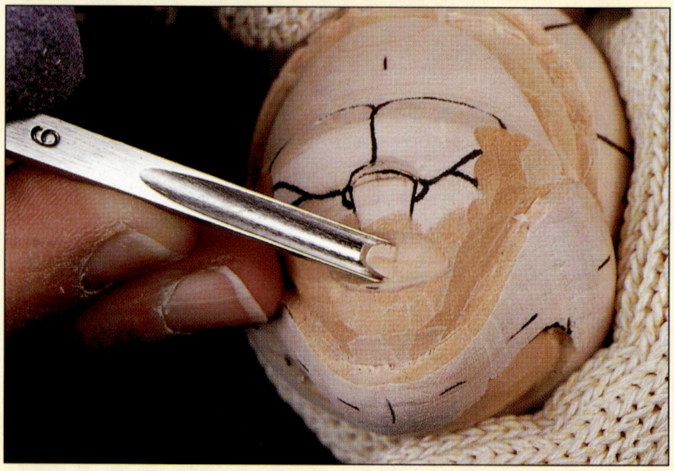

28 *Check that both sides at the temple area are equal.*

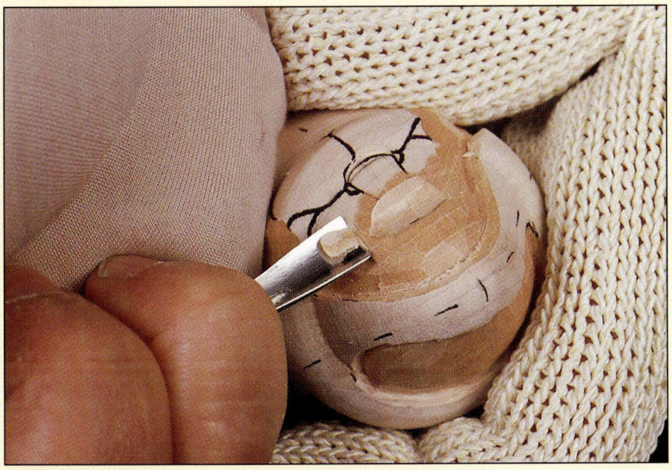

29 *I decided to come out farther onto the sides of the face with the larger U-gouge to narrow this portion.*

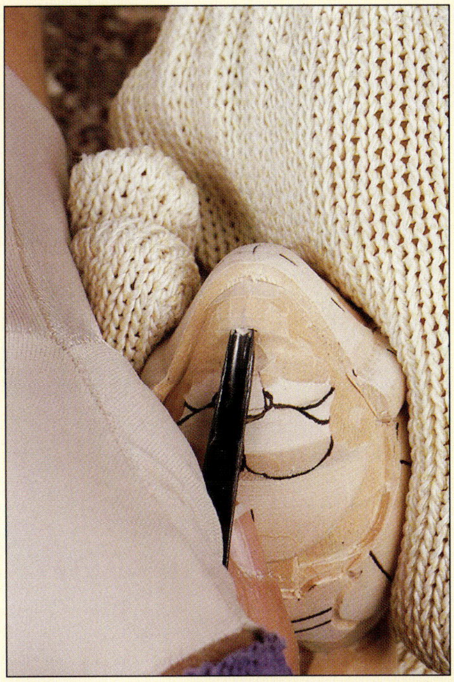

30 *Use a small u-gouge to carve a divot between the eyebrows.*

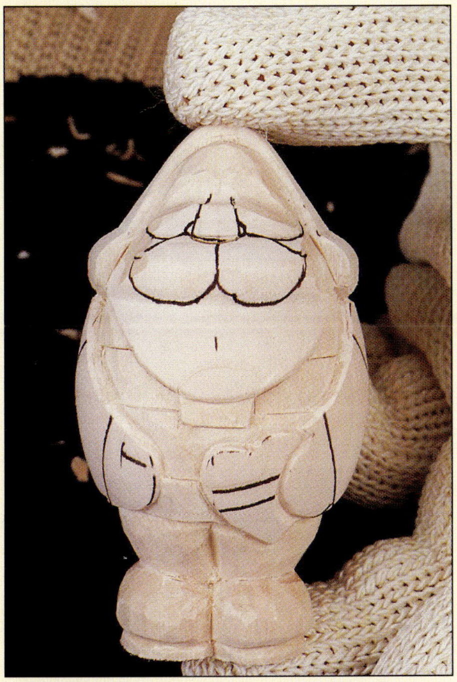

31 *This photo shows what your Santa should look like at this point.*

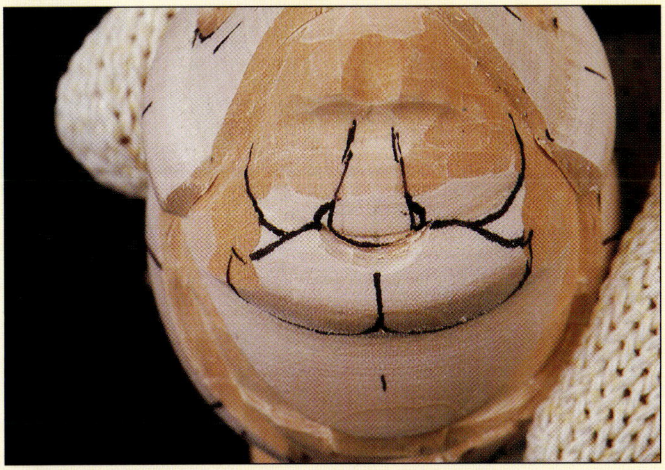

32 *Check to make sure that your cuts are clean.*

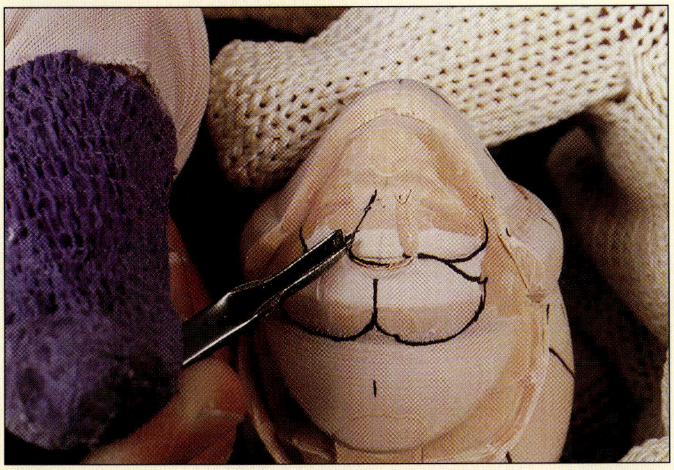

33 *V-tool from corner of the nose to the inside corner of eye.*

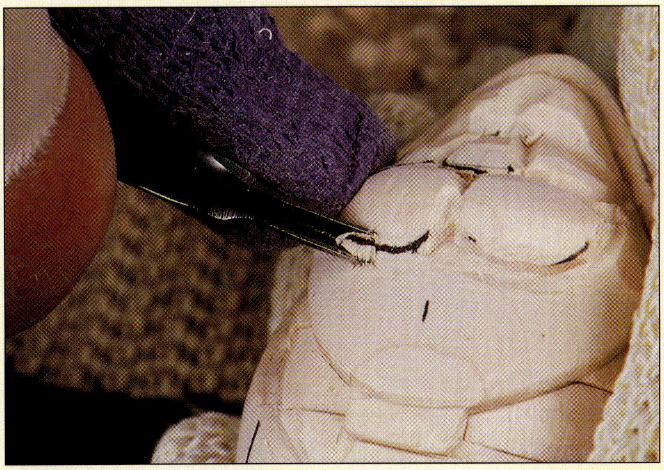

34 *V-tool a stop cut around the mustache.*

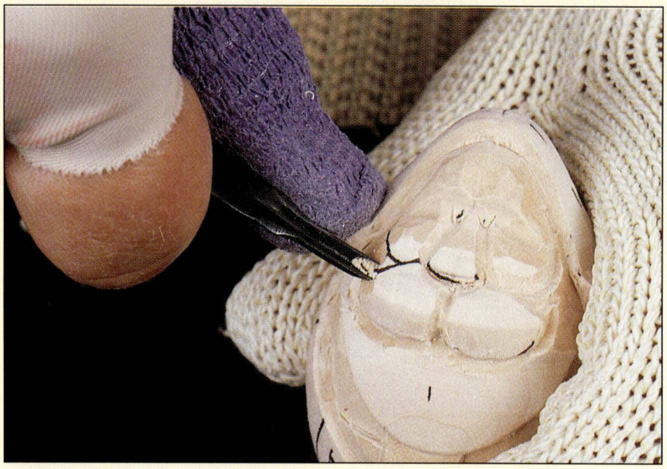

35 *Continue with the V-tool around the remainder of the mustache.*

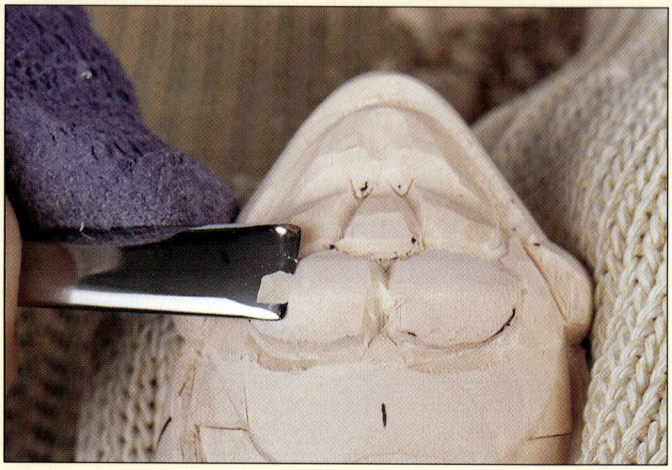

36 *Turn the sweep over to shape and carve the mustache.*

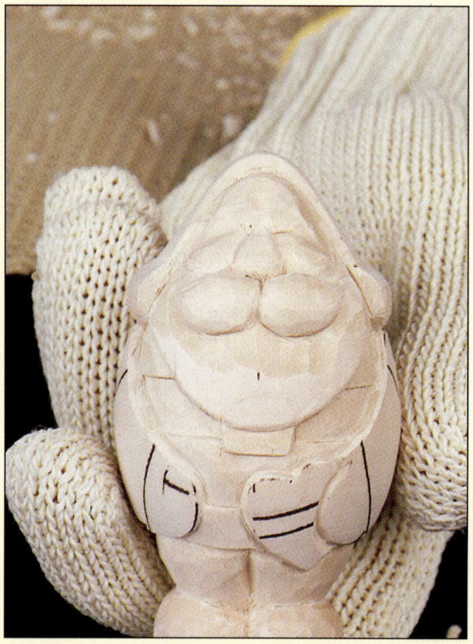

37 *Now is a good time to check the face for symmetry before continuing.*

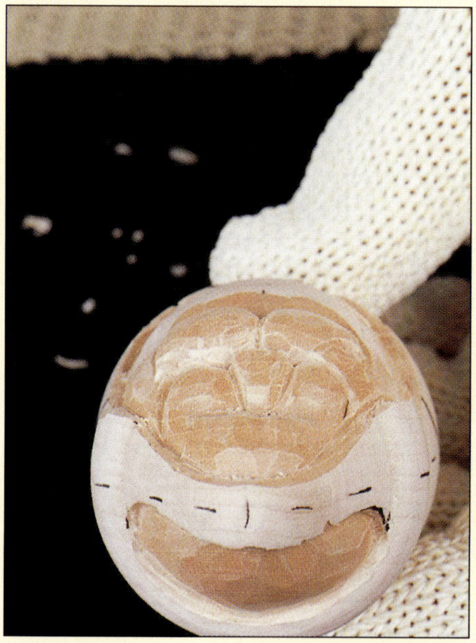

38 *Check for balance from the top view as well. This angle will help you to quickly spot any irregularities.*

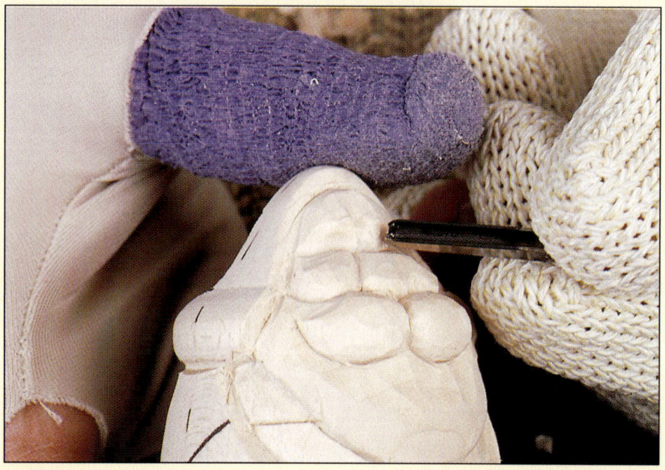

39 *Use a small u-gouge to carve the eye area lower than the adjacent nose.*

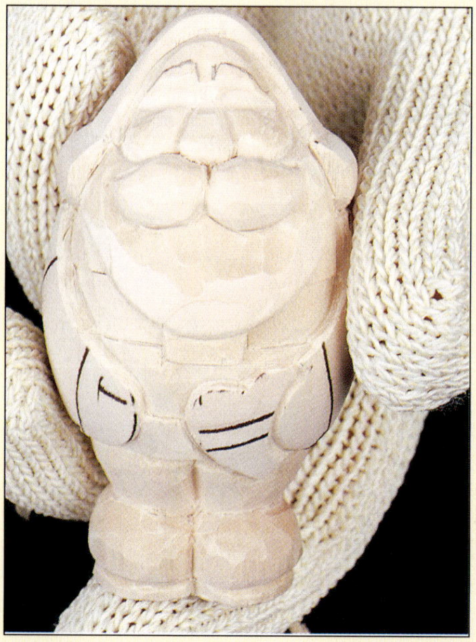

40 *Note the depth of the eye area. Draw the tops of the eyebrows.*

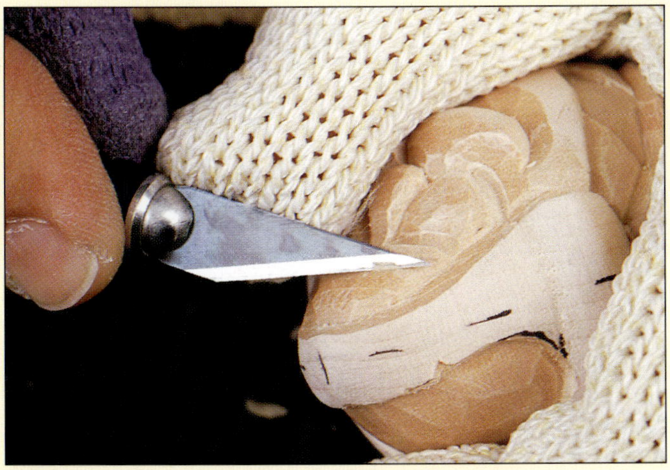

41 *Inert a new blade in the hobby knife and carve away the wood above the eyebrows. This allows the eyebrows to stand up without having to actually carve them.*

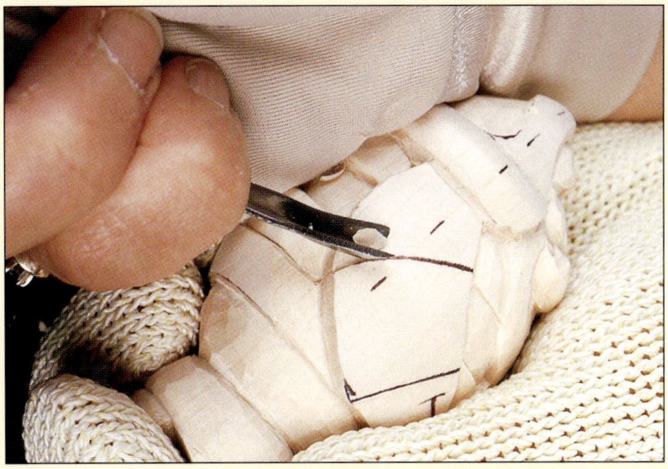

42 *Moving away from the face for a couple of minutes, lay the v-tool on its side and stop cut across the cuff.*

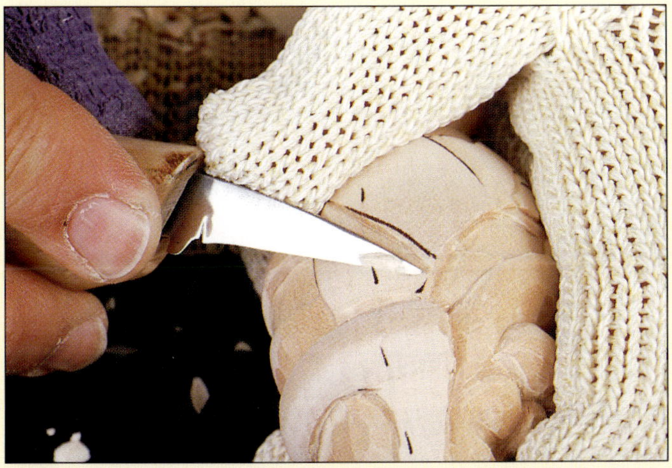

43 *Use a knife to remove all of the sanded surface of the sleeve so that the wood on the sleeve will be lower than that on the cuff.*

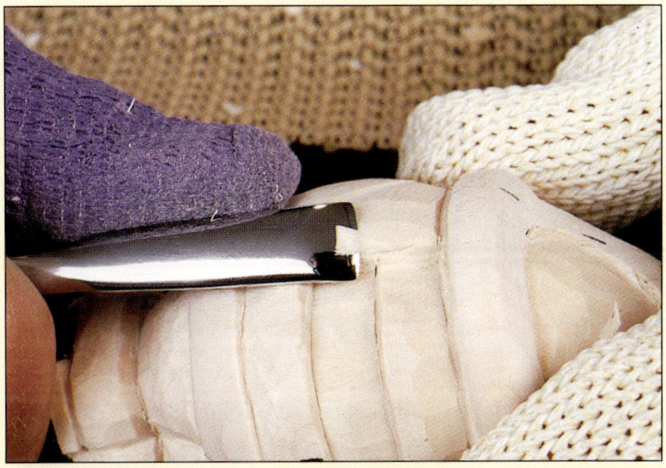

44 *Turn the sweep over and round off the corners on the sleeves.*

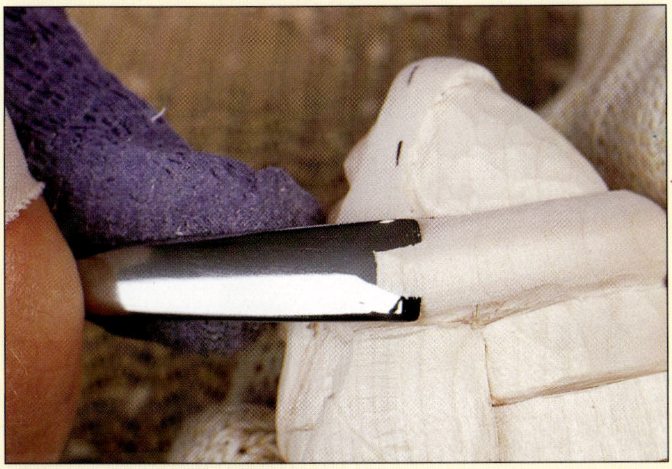

45 *Use the sweep in the same manner to remove the sanded surface of the hat's fur trim.*

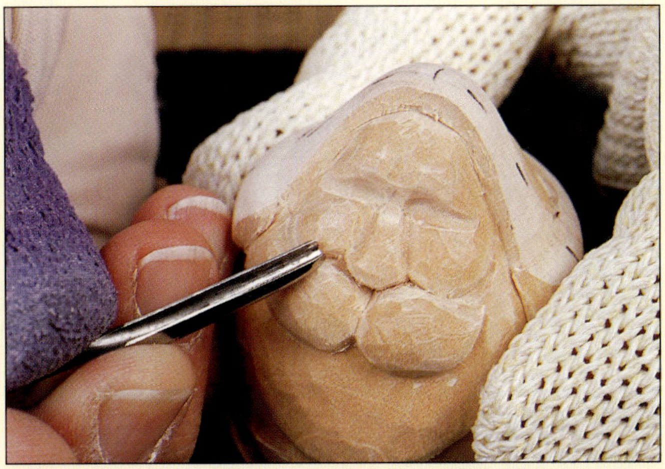

46 *Moving back to the face, I have used this small u-gouge to deepen the eye area.*

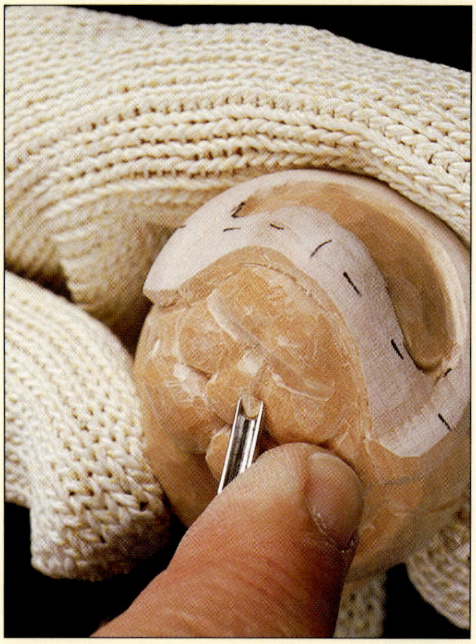

47 Using the u-gouge, start above the top side of the nostril and carve a ditch up to the inside corner of the eye. This will help to give the face more depth.

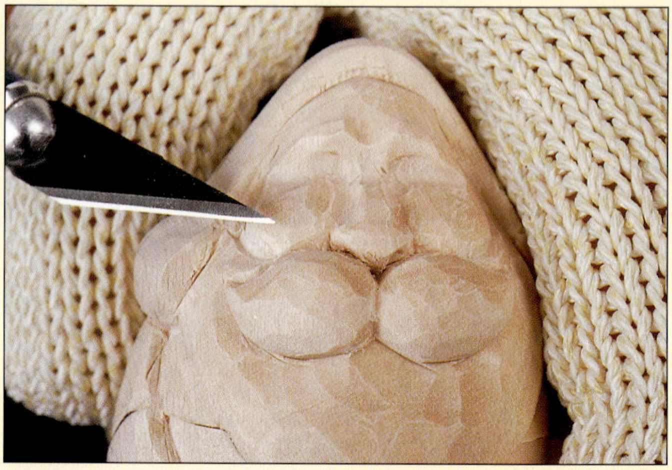

48 Remove a little wedge between the intersection of the nose-cheek-mustache area with a hobby knife. This cut will give shape to the outside corners of the nose. The nostrils may also be carved with the hobby knife.

49 Draw the thumb onto the mitten. Carve and separate the mitten from the cuff, again by using the v-tool on its side, allowing the cuff to remain higher than the back of the hand.

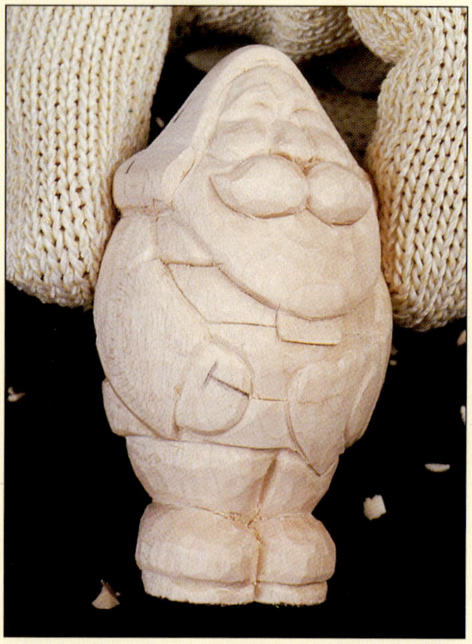

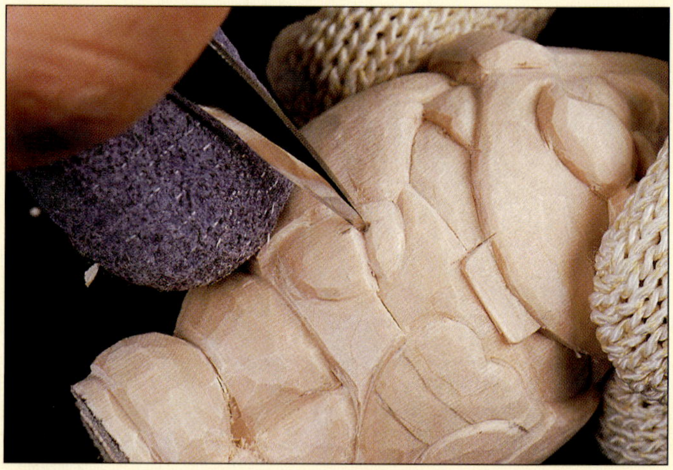

50 Stop cut straight into the crossed "T" and complete the thumb with a v-tool.

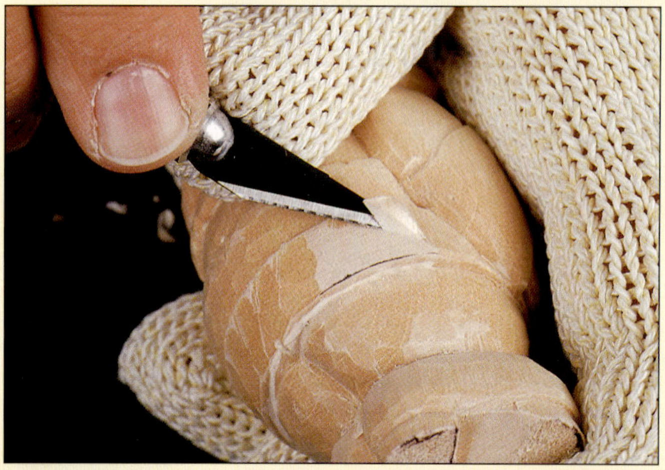

51 Remove all of the remaining sanded surfaces with a hobby knife.

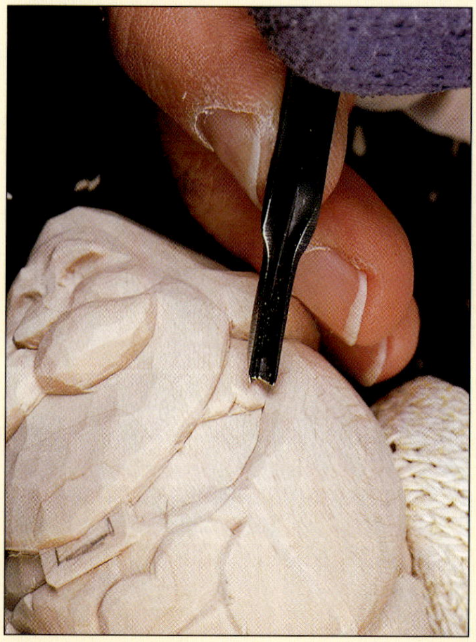

52 Use a v-tool to make the gathers in the clothing around the waist

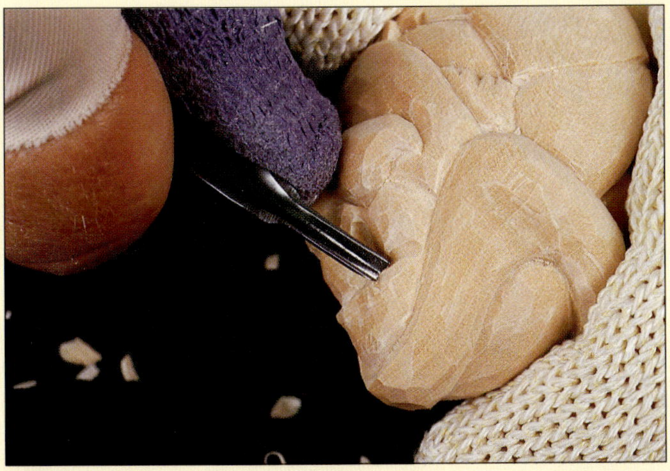

53 *Add details to the eyebrows with v-tool.*

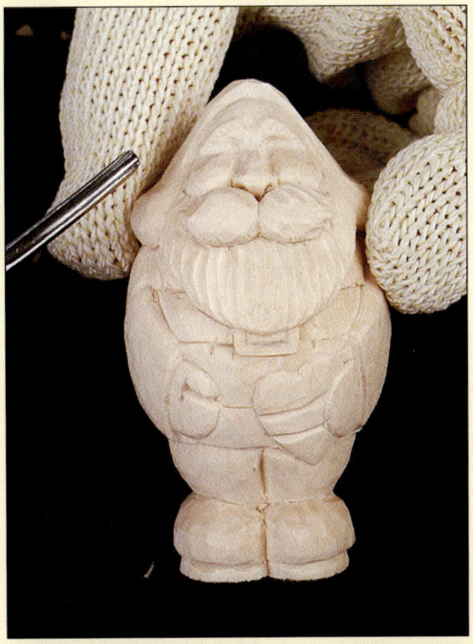

54 *Use a small u-gouge to add some interest to the beard.*

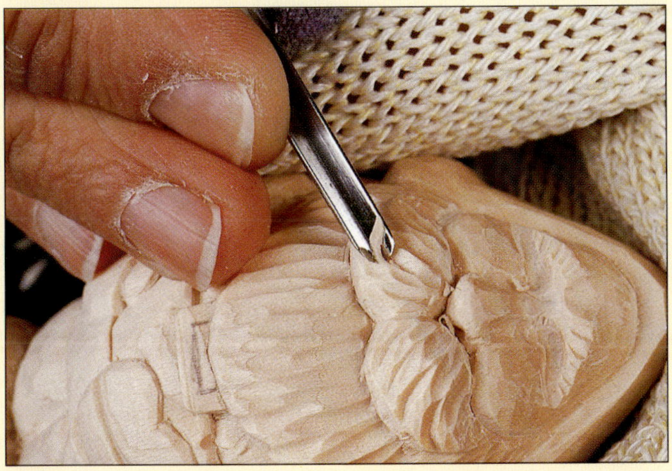

55 *Add more depth to the hair and the mustache with a v-tool.*

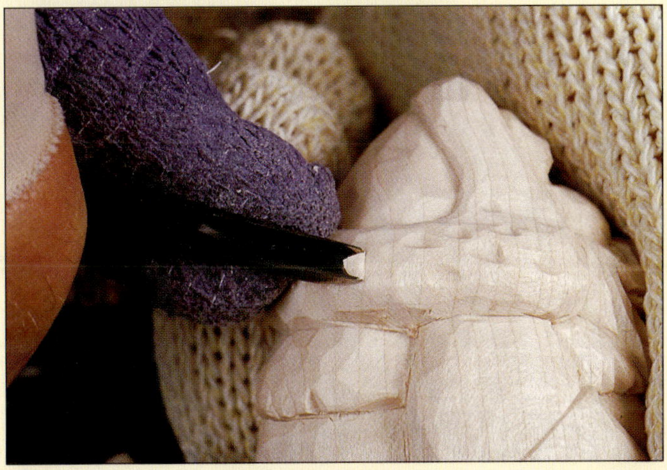

56 *Use a U-gouge to detail the fur trim*

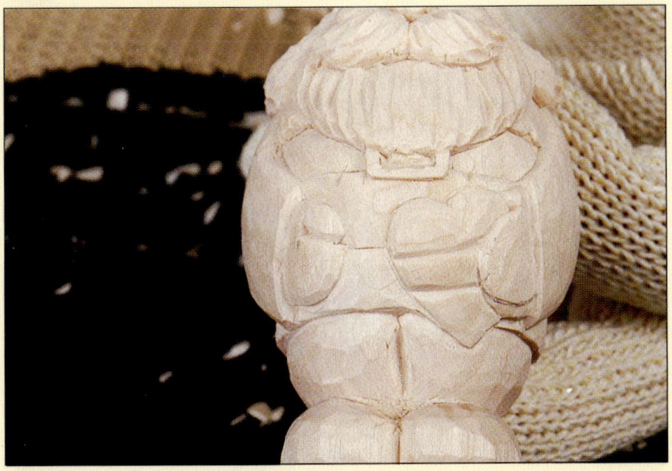

57 *Add detail to the belt and heart.*

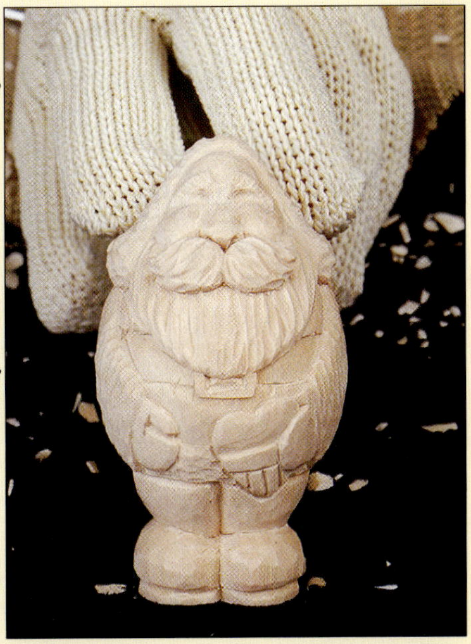

58 *Look over the carving, comparing one side to the other. Check for balance in features. Finish up your carving, making certain to remove all of the original sanded surfaces. Round off any sharp corners. If you are going to seal your work, now is a good time. I like to use Designs From The Heart Wood Sealer. Once your piece has dried completely, the final clean up of slivers is much easier. Rub over the surface of the grain with a wadded up brown paper grocery bag to remove any raised grain. Do not sand your piece.*

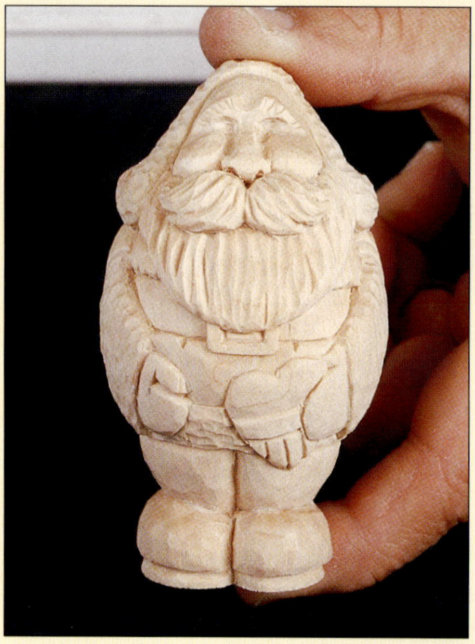

59 *The carving is now completed. It has been sealed and all the slivers have been removed.*

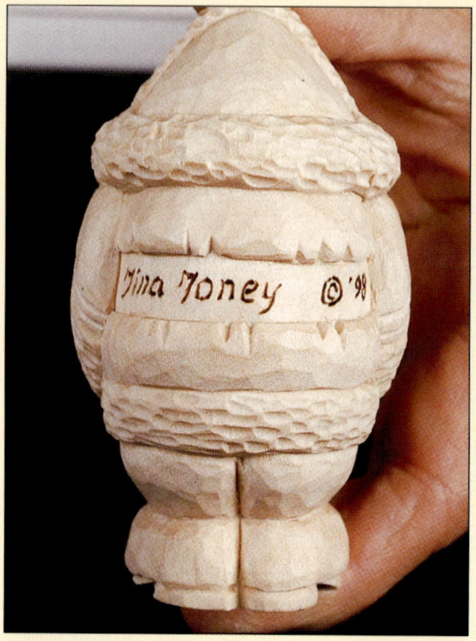

60 *I signed this piece using a woodburner. You can sign your work after the painting is completed and prior to the sealer being applied. If you are using a permanent pen, set the ink with a light misting of Deco Art Acrylic Sealer/Finisher Matte DAS13 before the final varnish is applied.*

PAINTING THE PROJECT SANTA

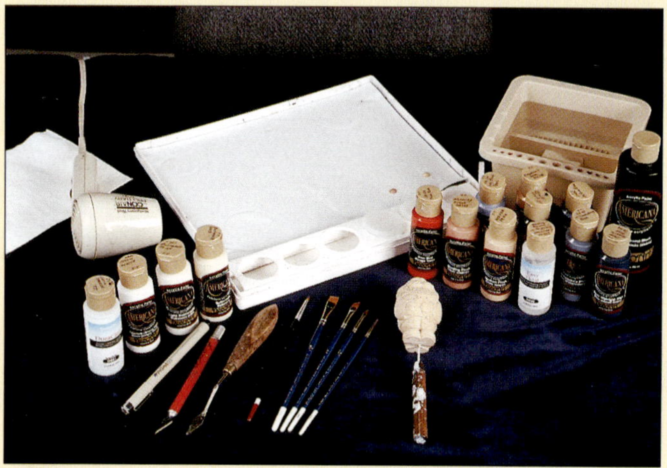

1 *To paint the Santa, you'll need a Sta-Wet palette, a hairdryer, paper towels, a water basin, a palette knife, a hobby knife, a Pigma Pen, and a stick to hold the Santa. I used various Betty Byrd angular and round brushes and a Pat Godin blending brush to paint this piece.*

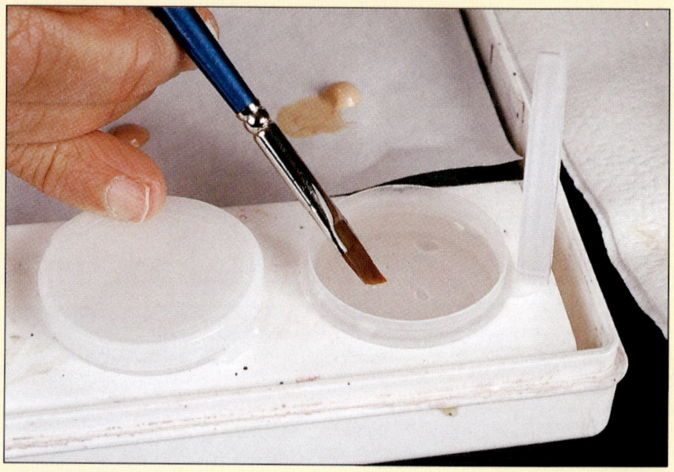

2 *Mix Deco Art™ Easy Float with clean water for more control over the paint. This also allows the paint to flow smoothly onto the wood and prevents ridges from forming.*

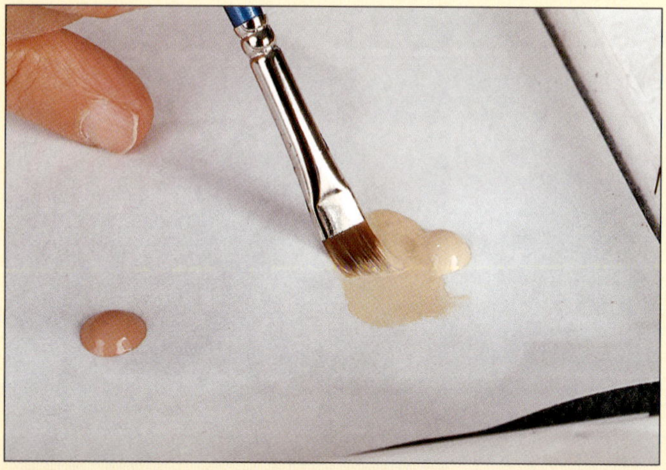

3 *Pick up some of the Medium Flesh color on your brush. Work the brush across the palette several times to spread the paint evenly in the bristles.*

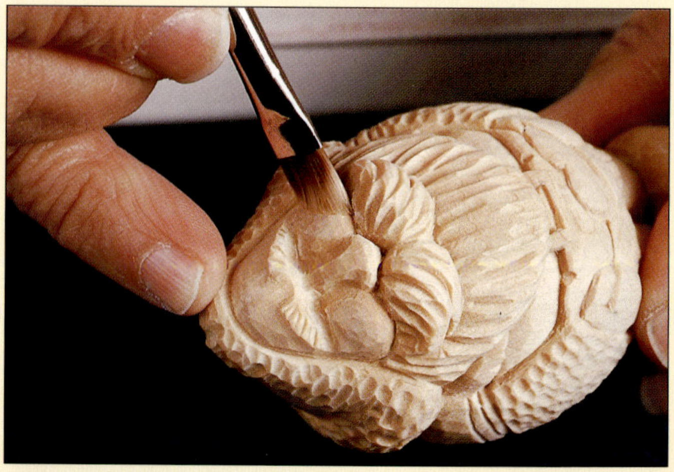

4 *Apply the Medium Flesh over all to the face. It doesn't hurt to apply this over the eye area or eyebrows, but try to avoid adjacent areas.*

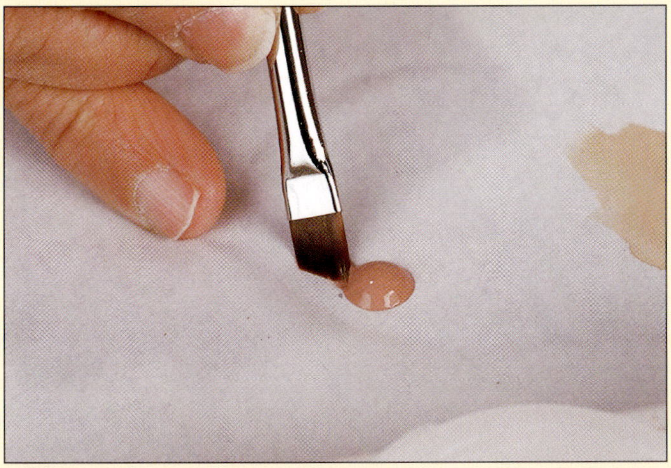

5 *Swish the brush clean in the big brush basin, dip the brush into the small basin with the Easy Float, pat once on a paper towel, then corner load into the Shading Flesh.*

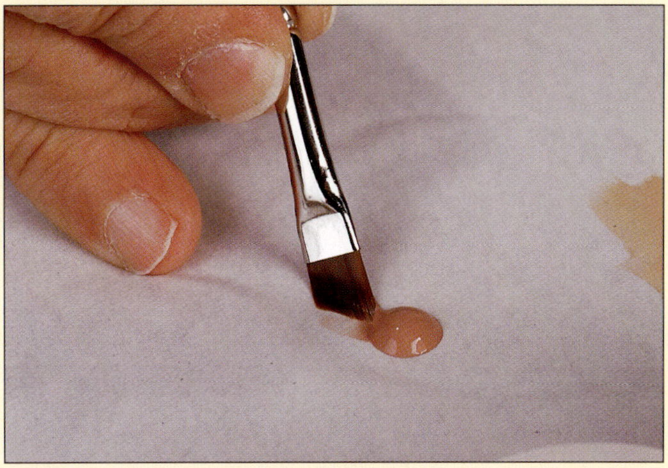

6 *Pull the paintbrush out of the puddle.*

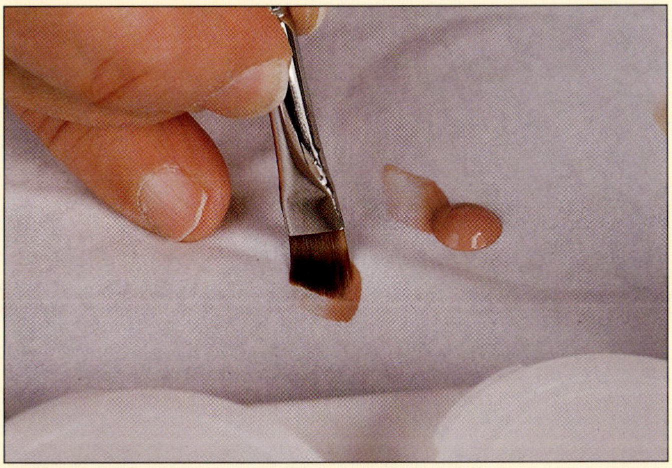

7 *Work the paint until it blends into the brush.*

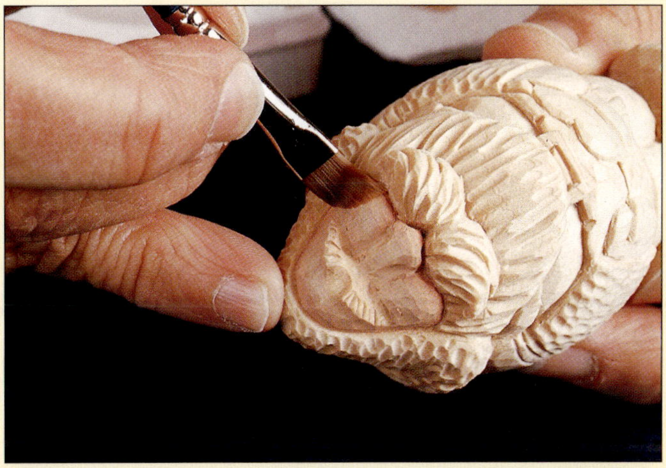

8 *Apply the Shading Flesh around the cheeks and the hairline.*

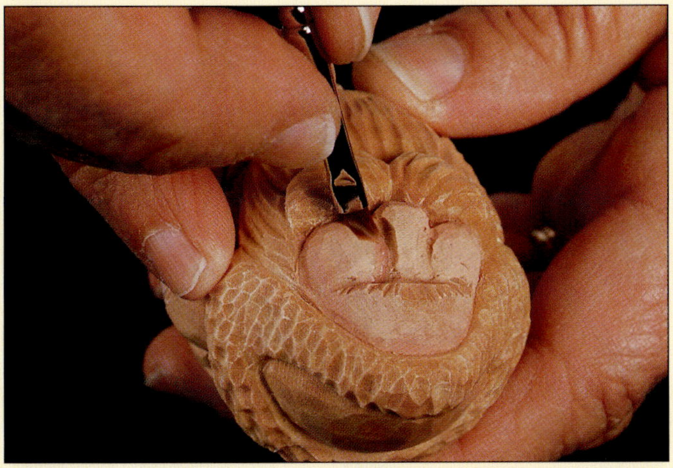

9 *Use a smaller angular shader to apply shading around the nose.*

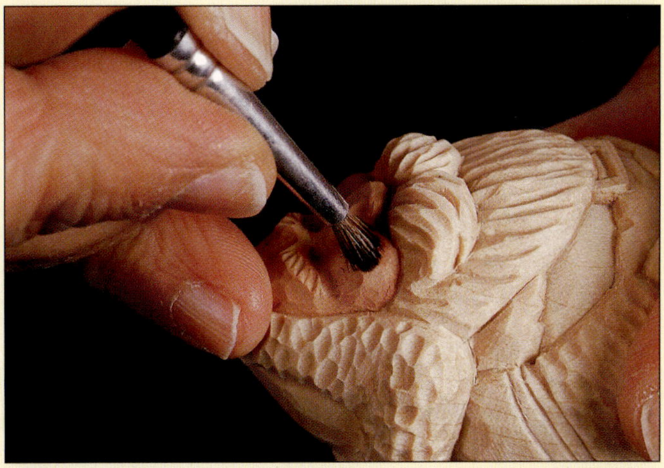

10 *A blending brush is used to stipple DeLane's Cheek color onto the cheeks.*

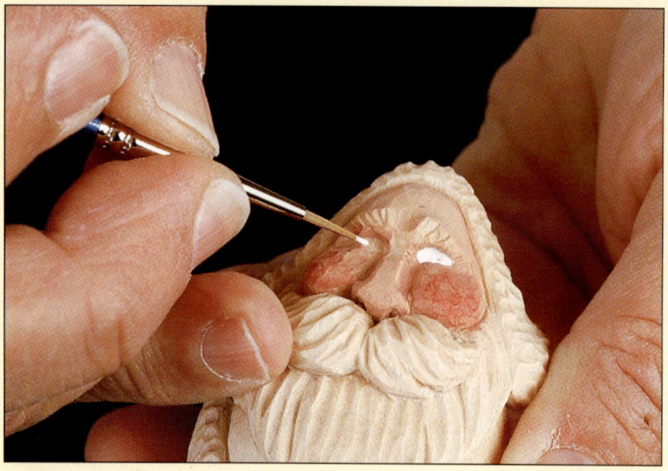

11 *Apply white to the eyes using a 00 or smaller round detail brush.*

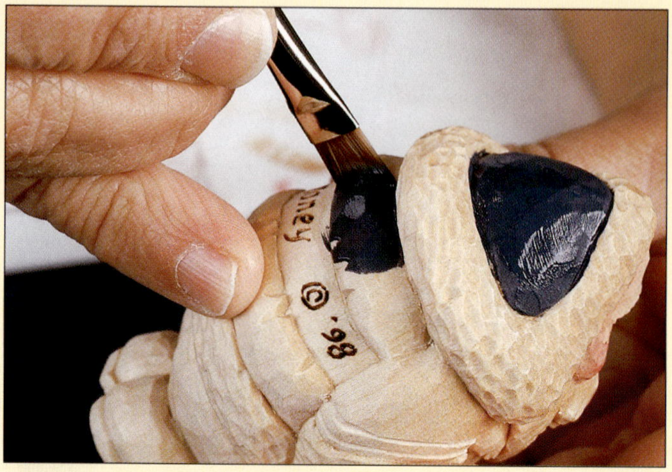

12 *Use a 1/4" angular shader to apply Uniform Blue to Santa's clothing.*

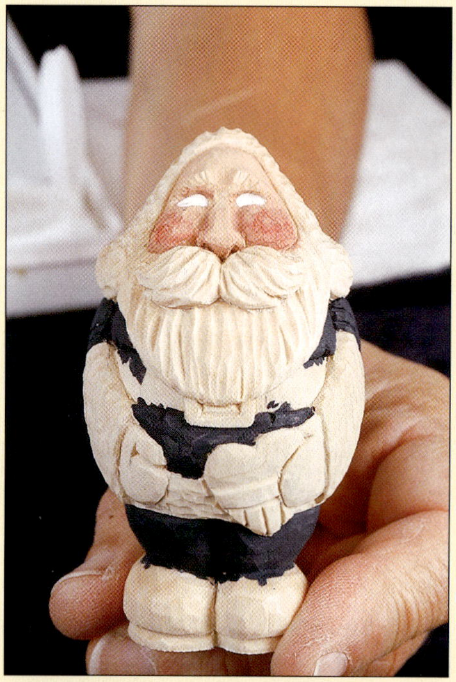

13 *Paint the pants, hat and coat.*

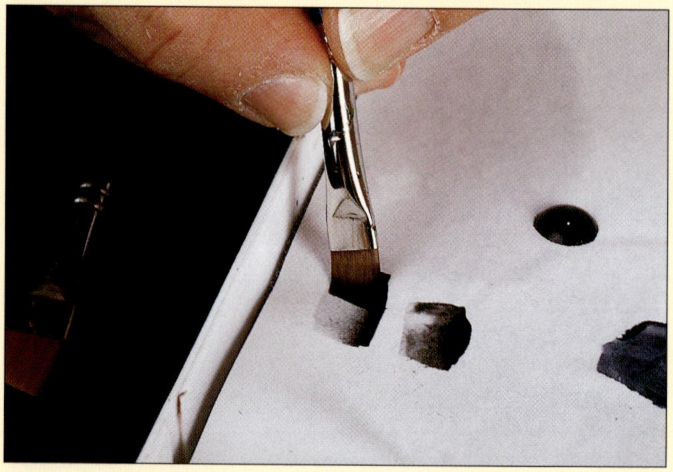

14 *Using Easy Float in the brush, lightly stroke it across a paper towel to remove any excess medium. Then load the brush with Lamp Black and blend the color on the palette.*

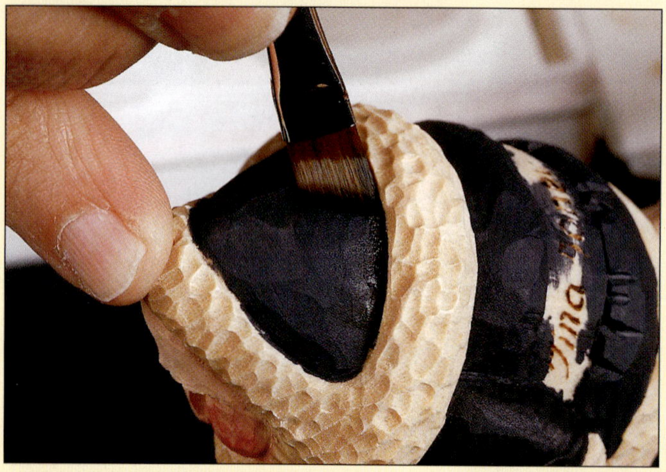

15 *Apply Lamp Black adjacent to the fur trim around the hat and shade all of the other areas adjacent to the arms, the belt, the fur trim of coat and the pants.*

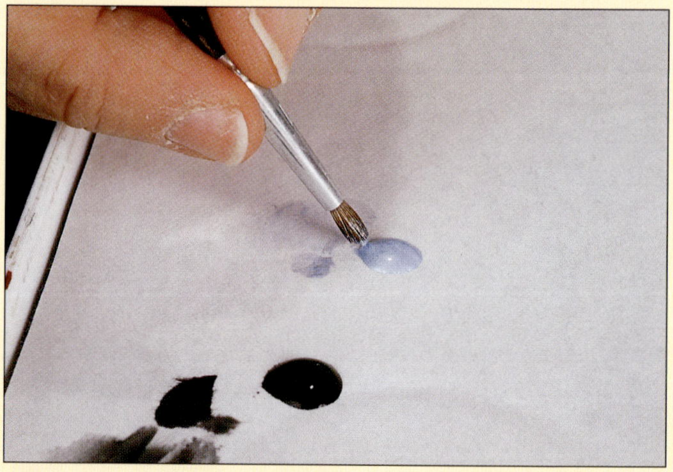

16 *Load Sky Blue Pearl into the blending brush.*

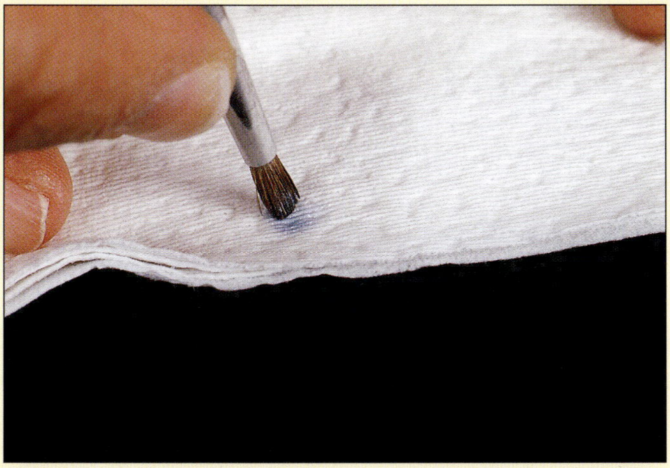

17 *Scrub most of the paint off onto the paper towel—a necessity when drybrushing.*

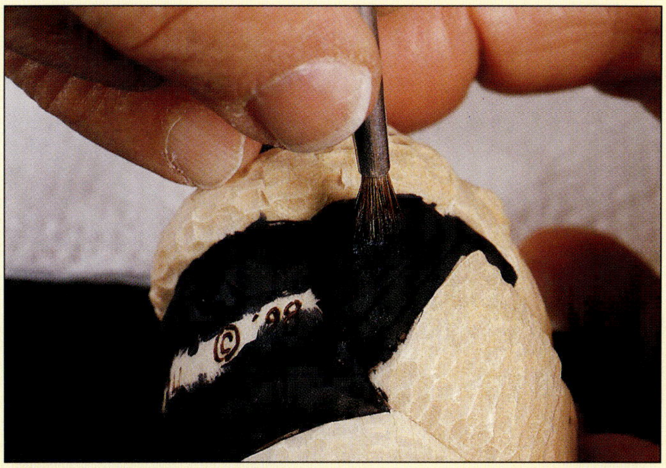

18 *Use the brush in a pouncing motion on the high spots. Be careful not to go into the shaded areas.*

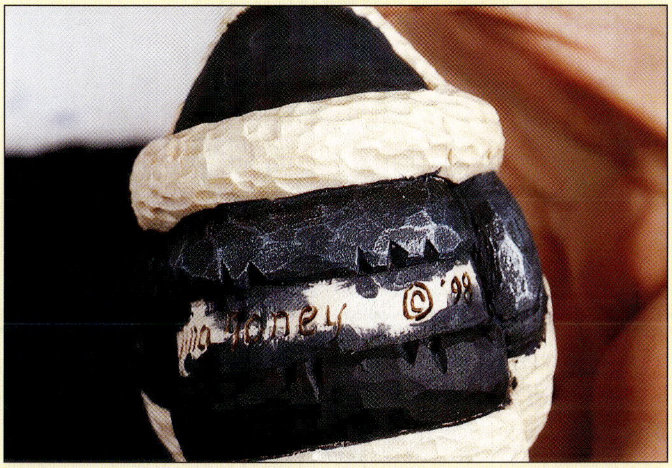

19 *This photo shows the drybrushed clothing. Notice how flat the pants area is compared to the remainder of the clothing.*

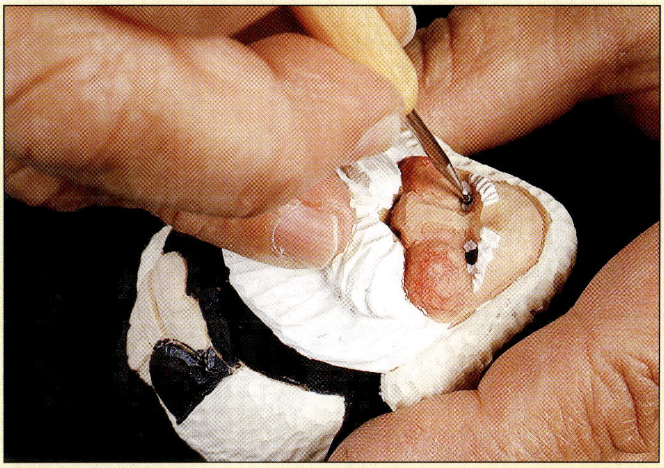

20 *Use a stylus to apply the eye color. Paint the eyes the same as the clothing, then add a smaller black pupil. Finish painting the remainder of the clothing and the heart.*

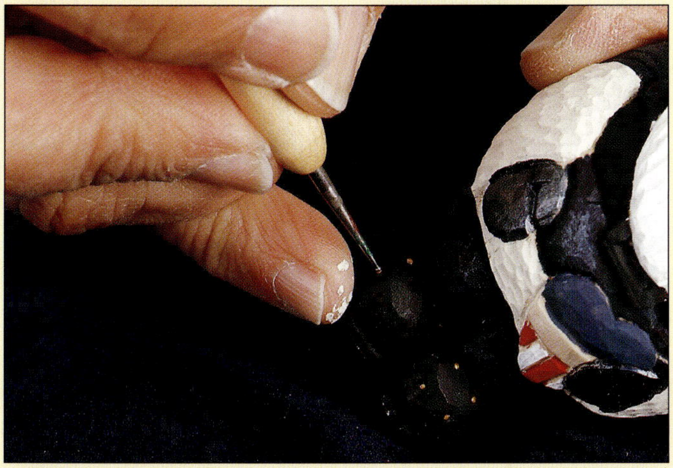

21 *Using the stylus again, apply Emperor's Gold to the buttons on the boots.*

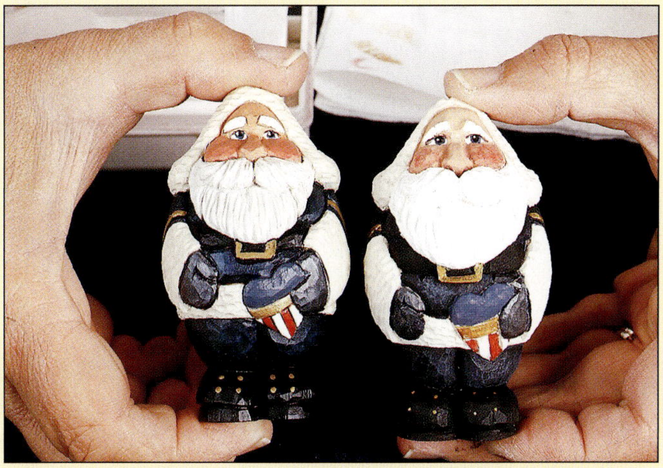

22 *The Santa on the left is finished. The top eyelid has been inked with the Pigma .005 permanent black pen and a matte sealer has been applied. The Santa on the right is the project piece carved and painted in this book. Notice how flat the paint appears prior to the application of the matte sealer.*

SANTA IN BLUE JEANS

Carved on Curtain Rod Finial Shape BTFO–01B

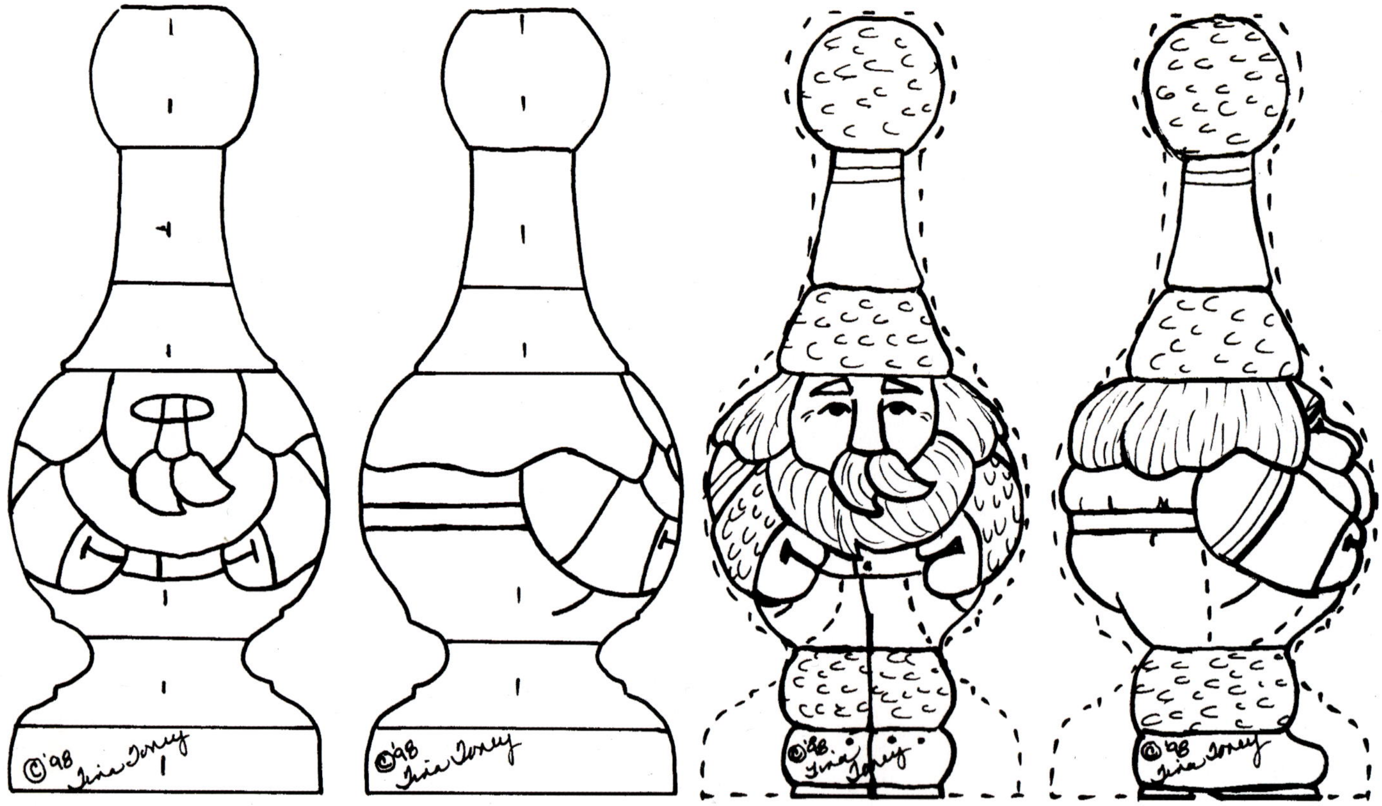

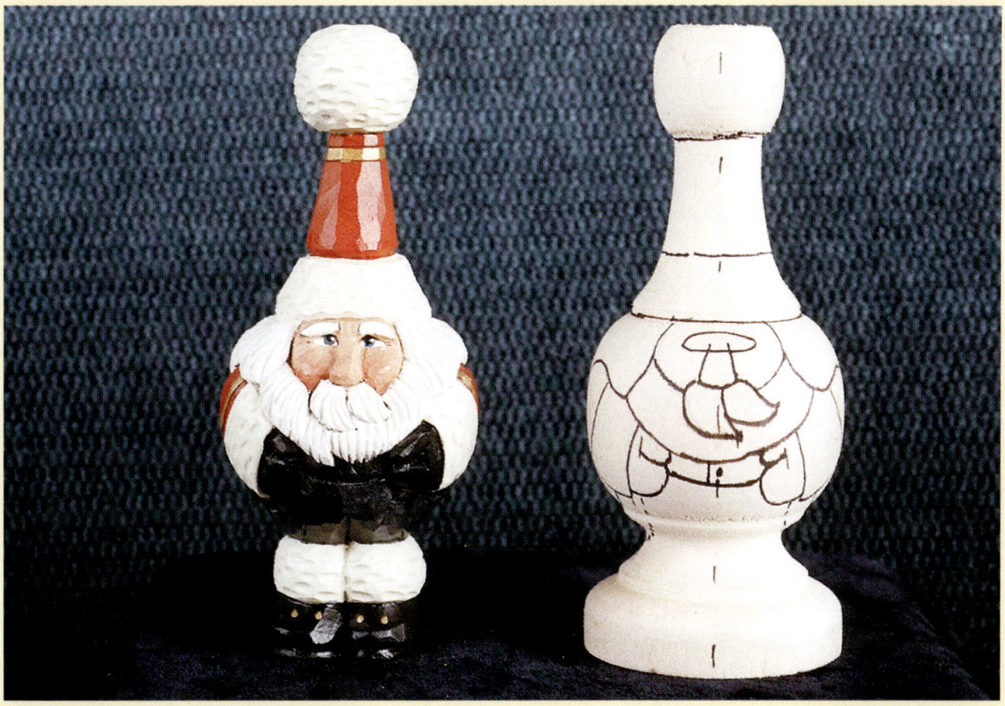

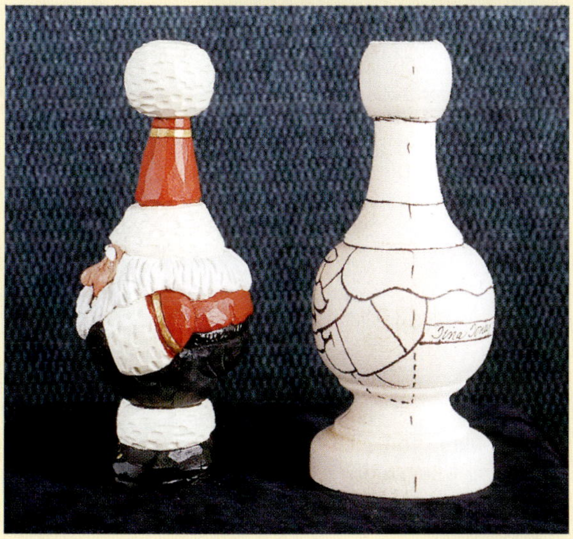

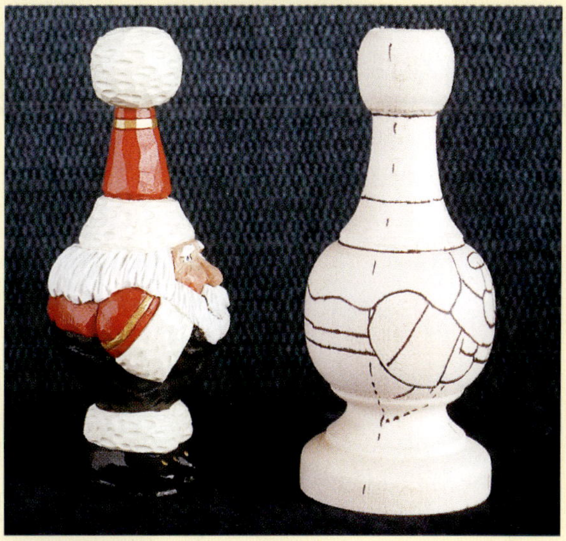

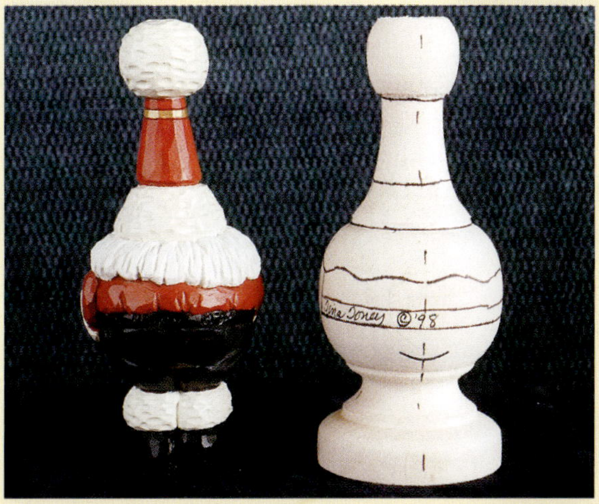

Oakie Santa

Carved on Acorn Shape #BTO-12

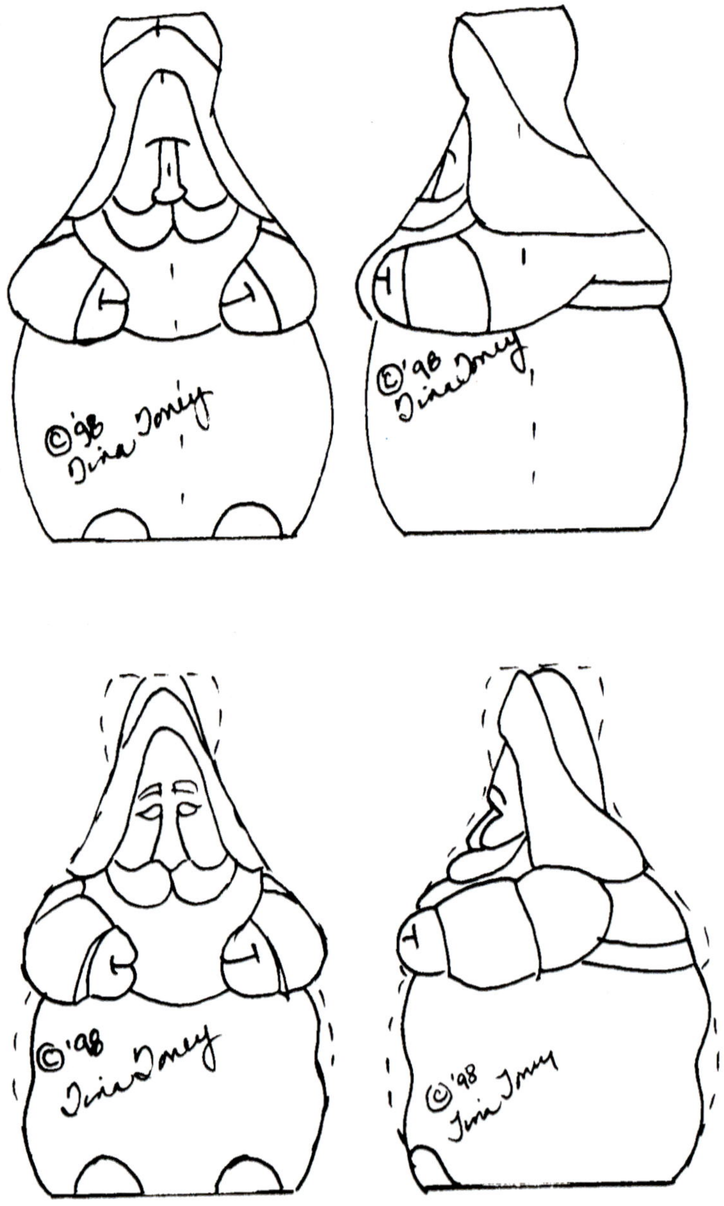

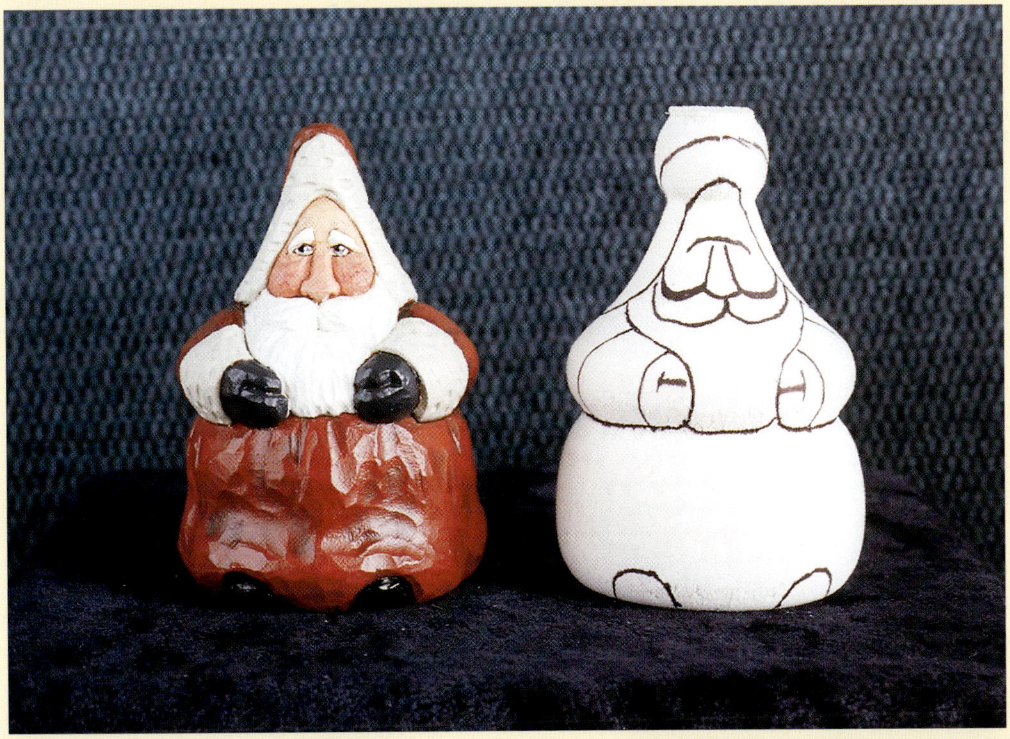

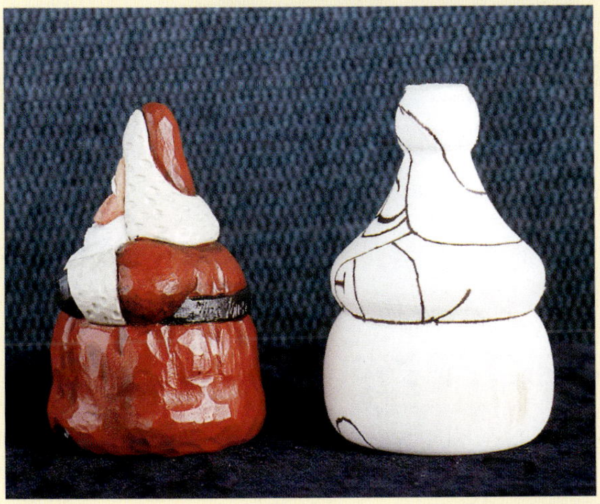

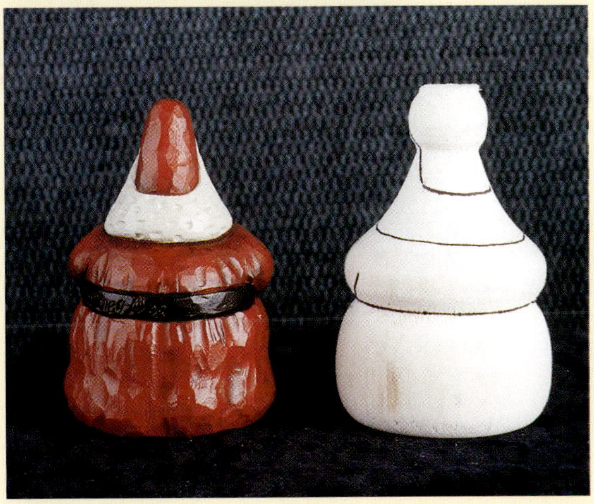

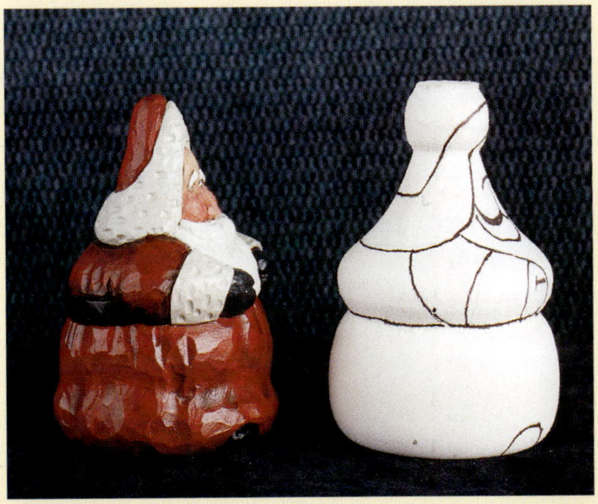

Grandfather Frost

Carved on Footed Egg Product #TT-01

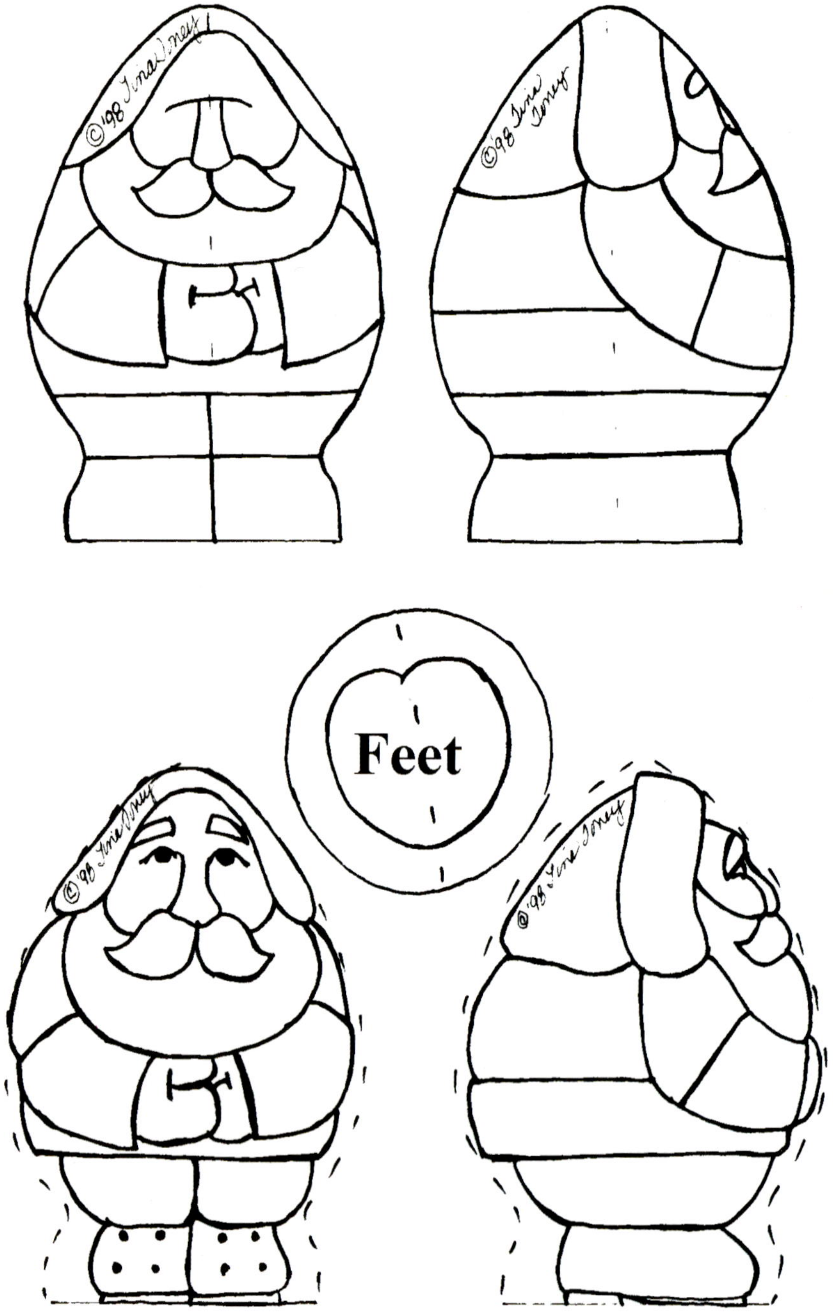

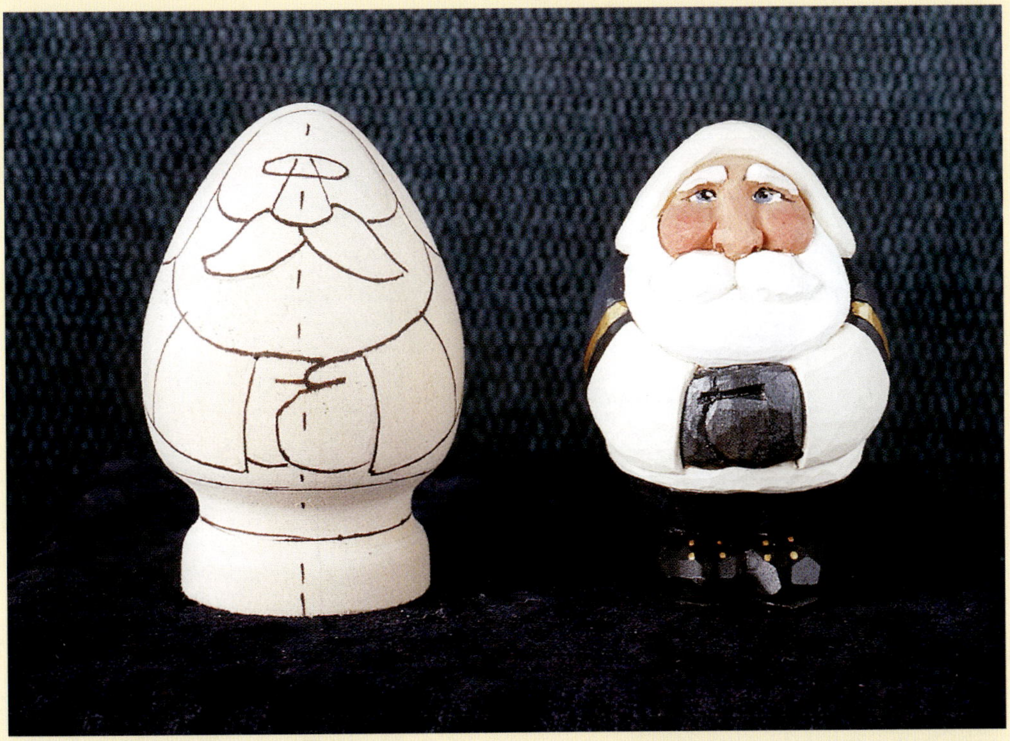

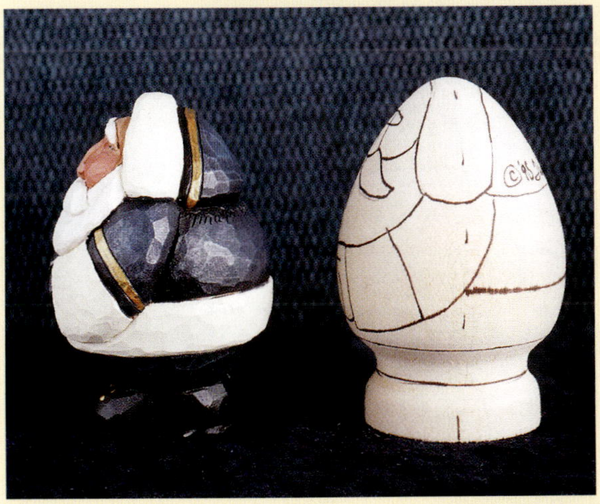

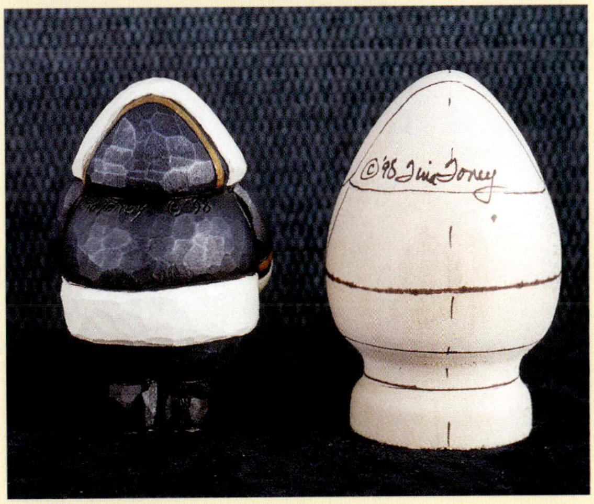

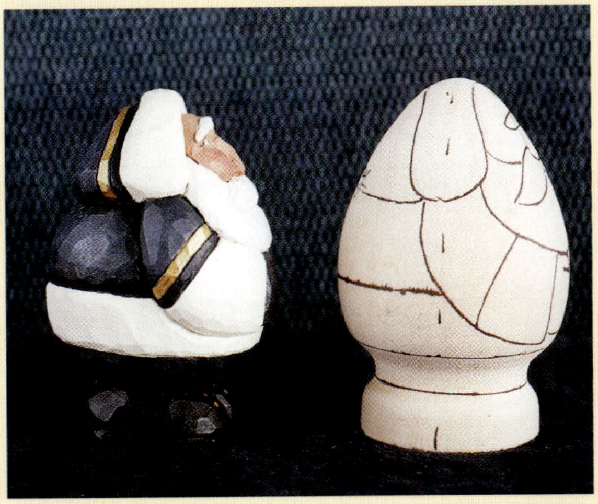

SNOWMAN

Carved on Bottle Shape #BTSN-28

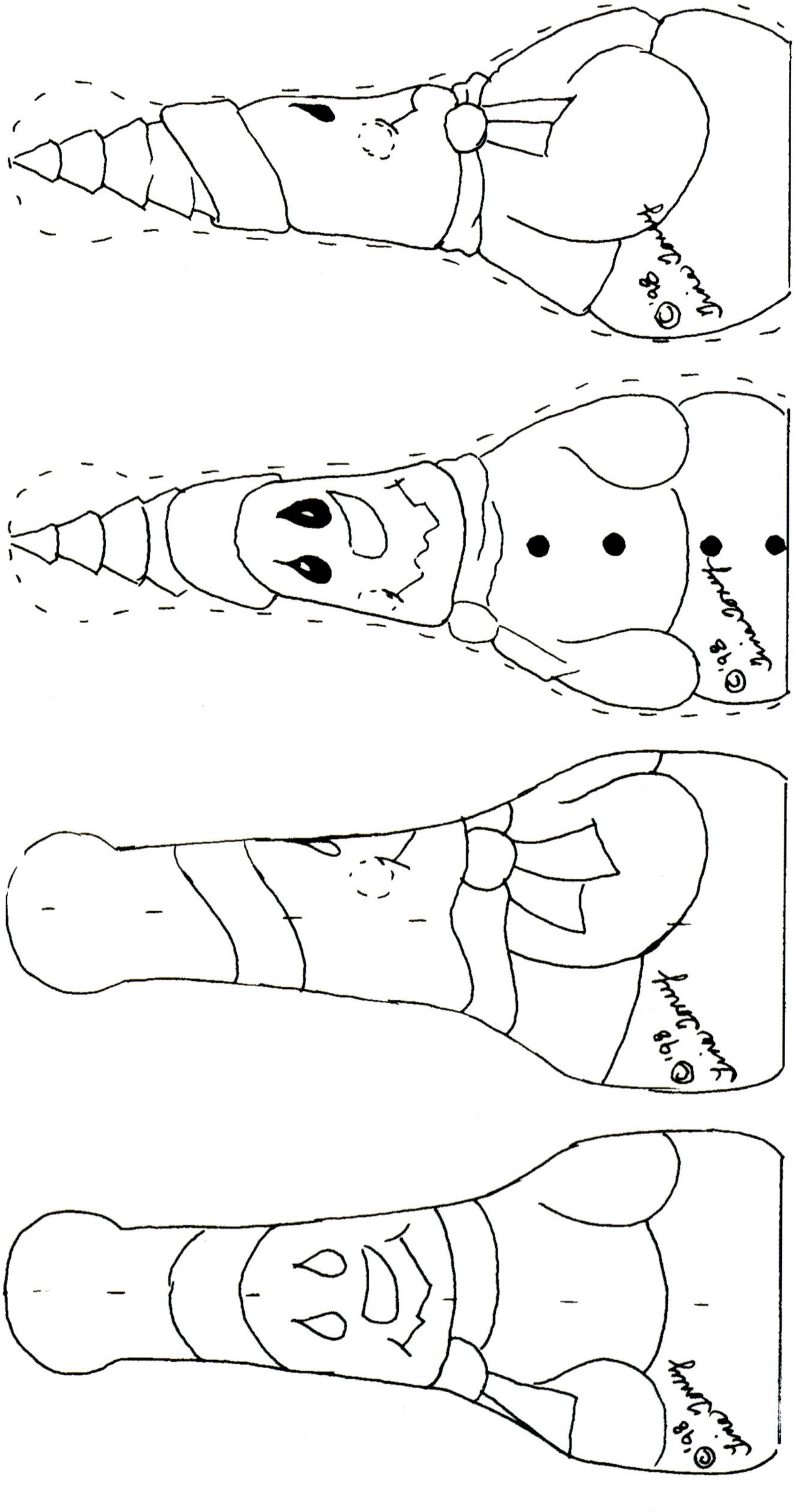

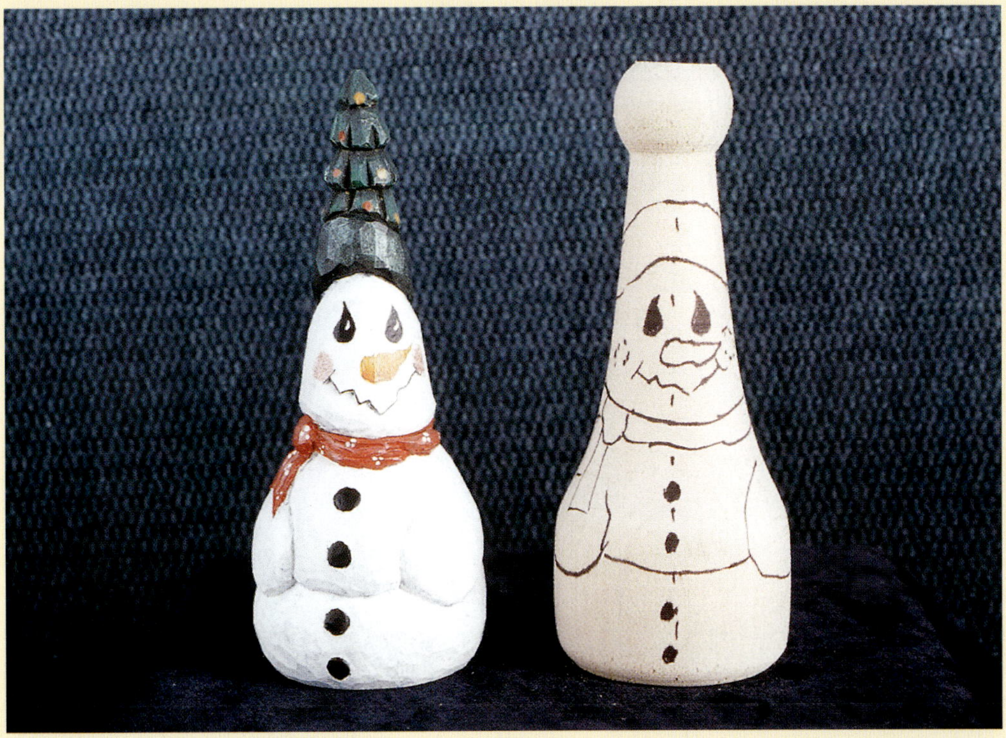

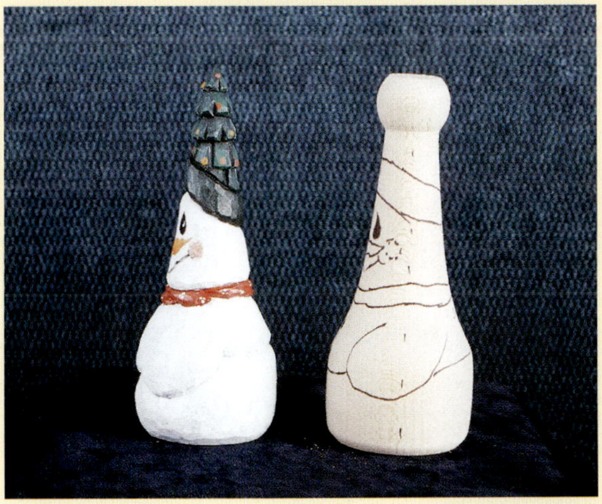

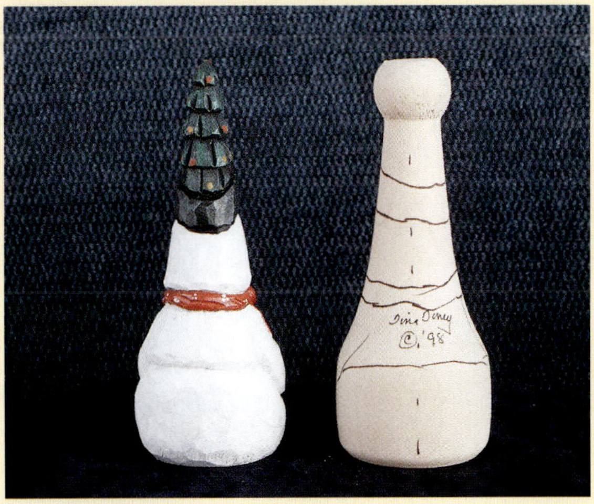

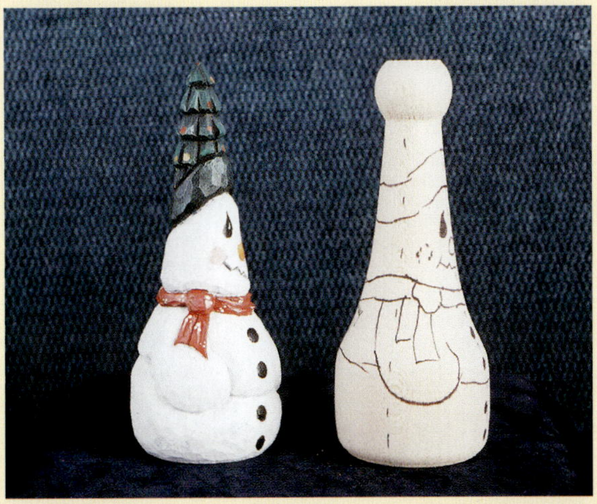

Icicle Santa

Carved on Icicle Shape #BTSN-27

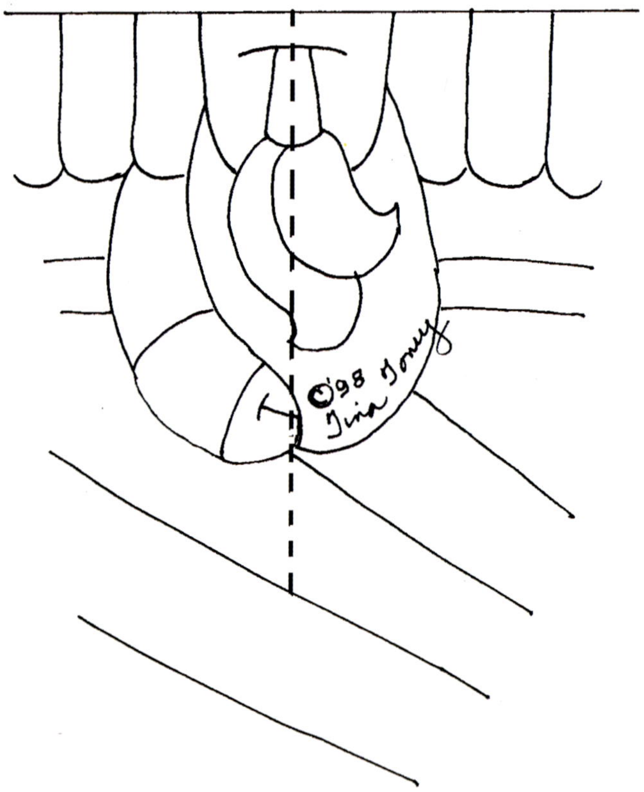

Special Instructions: Copy this pattern to tracing paper and transfer it onto the turning using graphite paper. Locate the center of the growth ring arches, which mark the center of the face. Place the top of the pattern below the larger bulge of the icicle turning, lining up the dotted lines with the center of the growth rings.

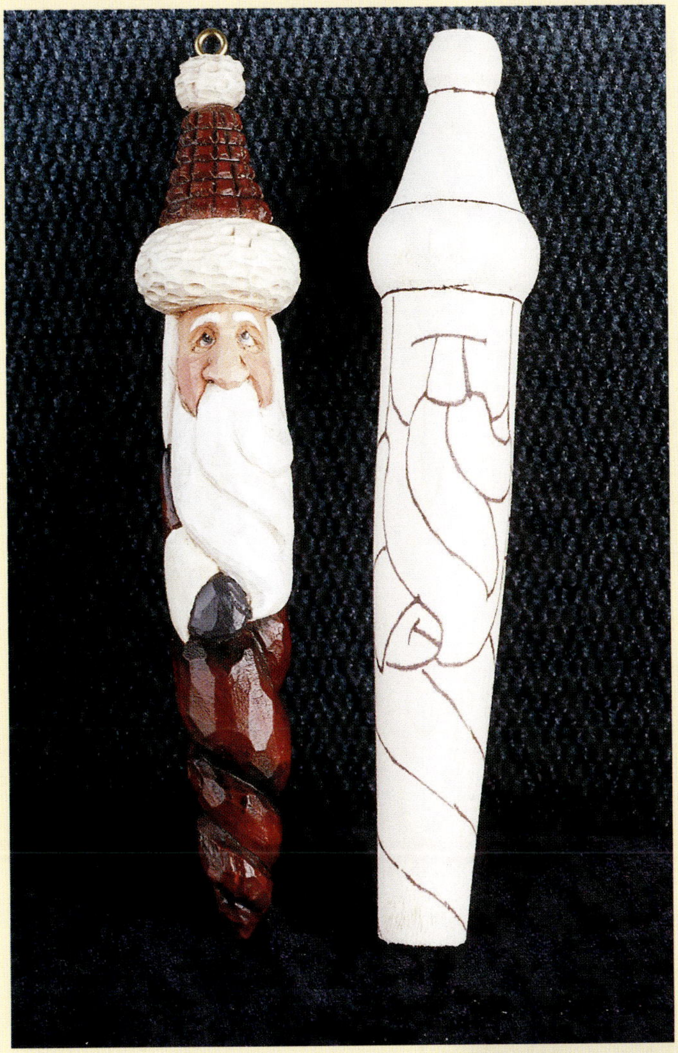

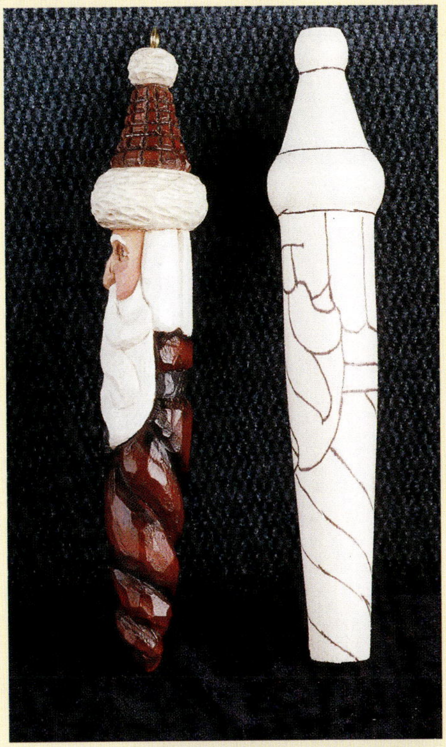

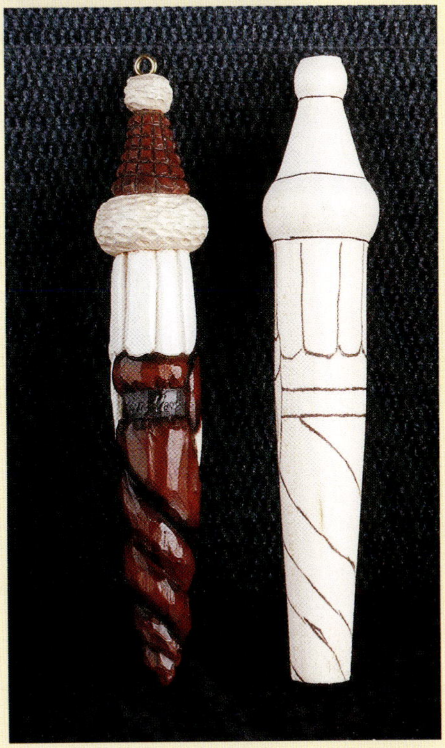

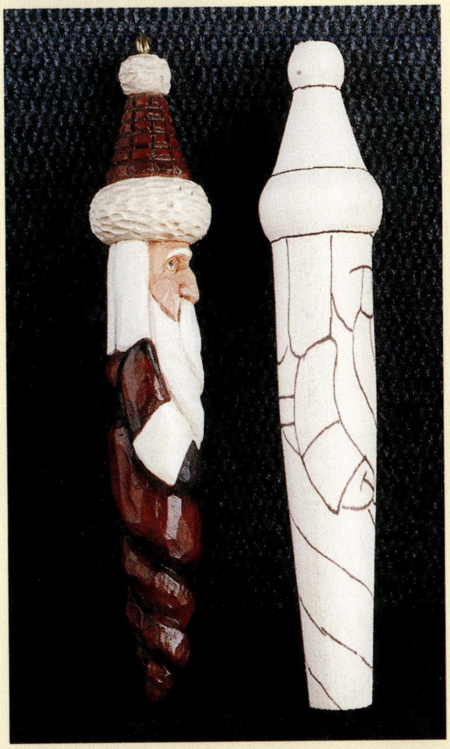

CHUBBY CHEEKS

Carved on Ginger Jar Shape #BTSN-26

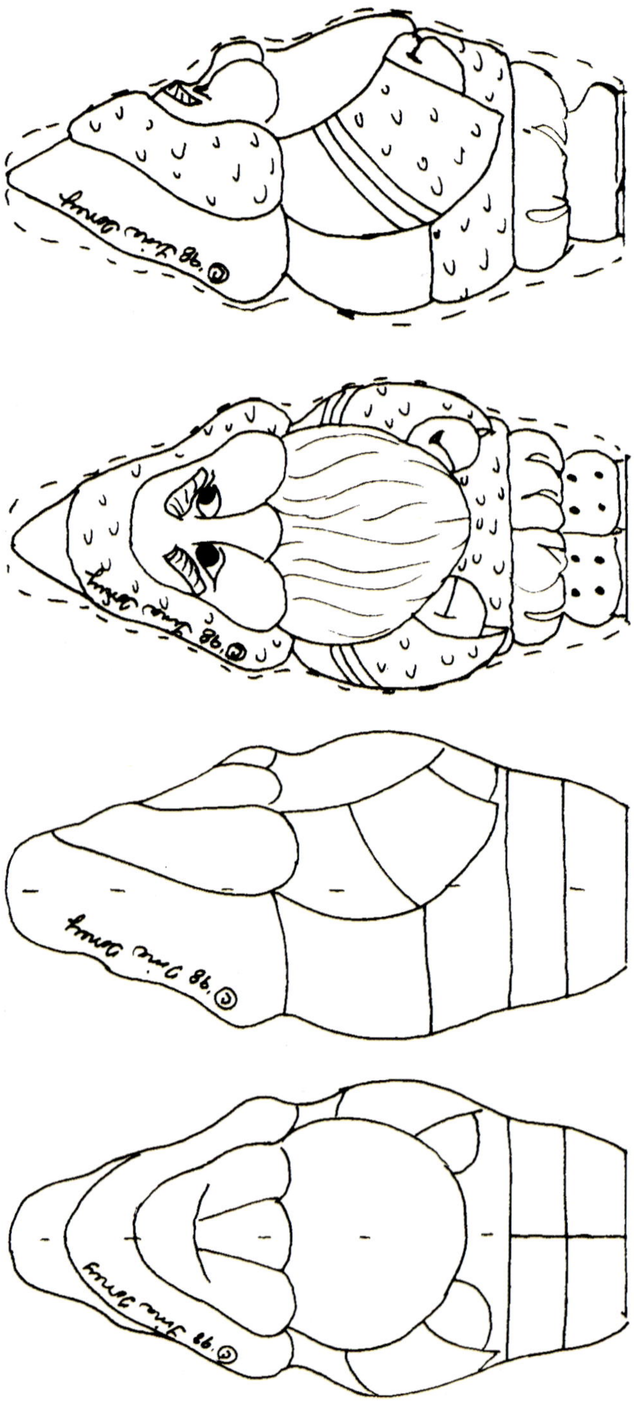

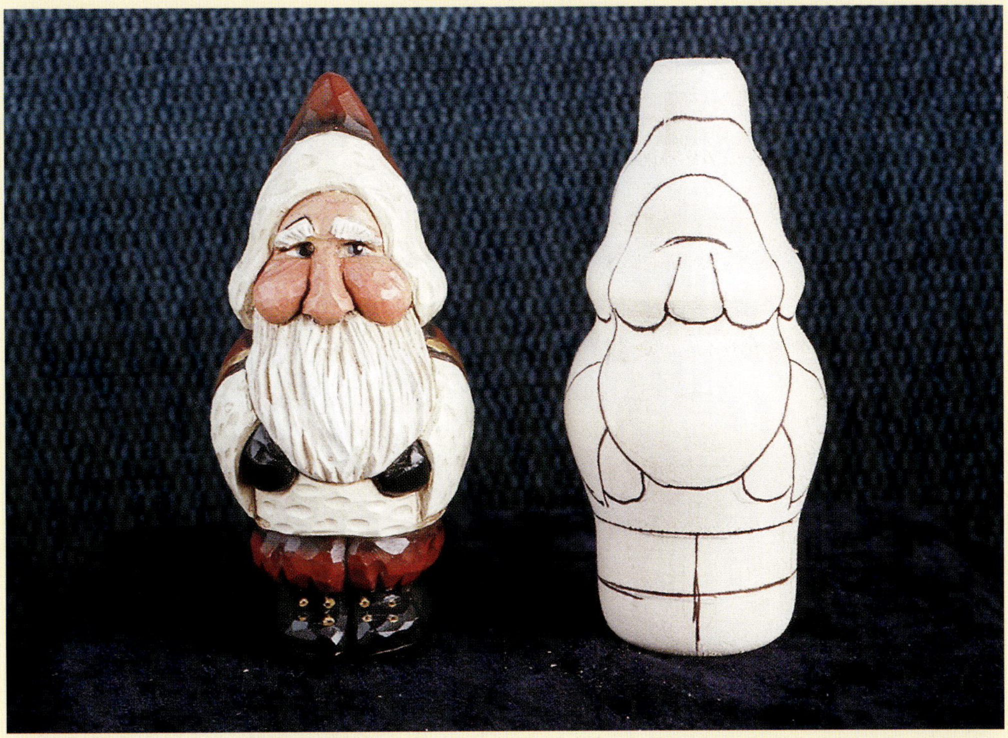

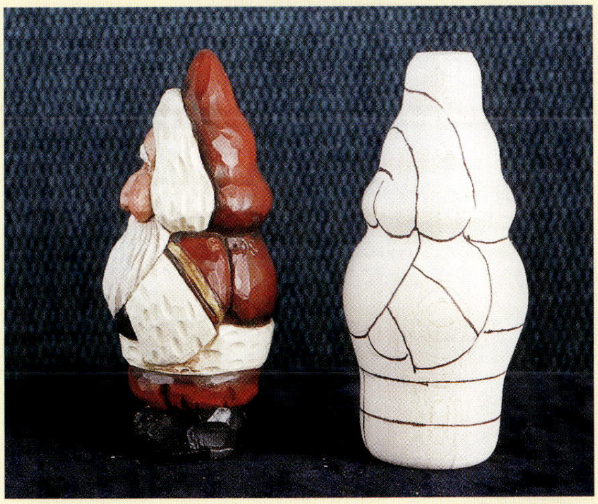

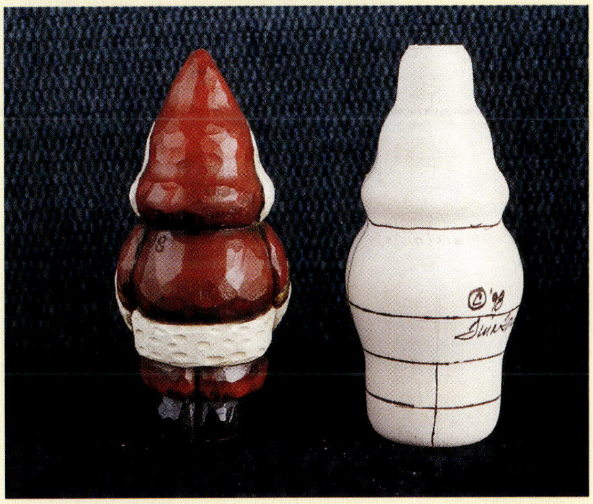

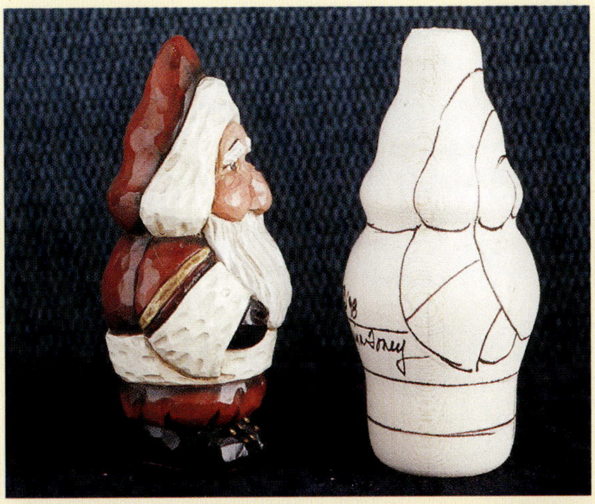

Chef Burgerfrier

Carved on Mini Bowling Pin Product #BTP-02

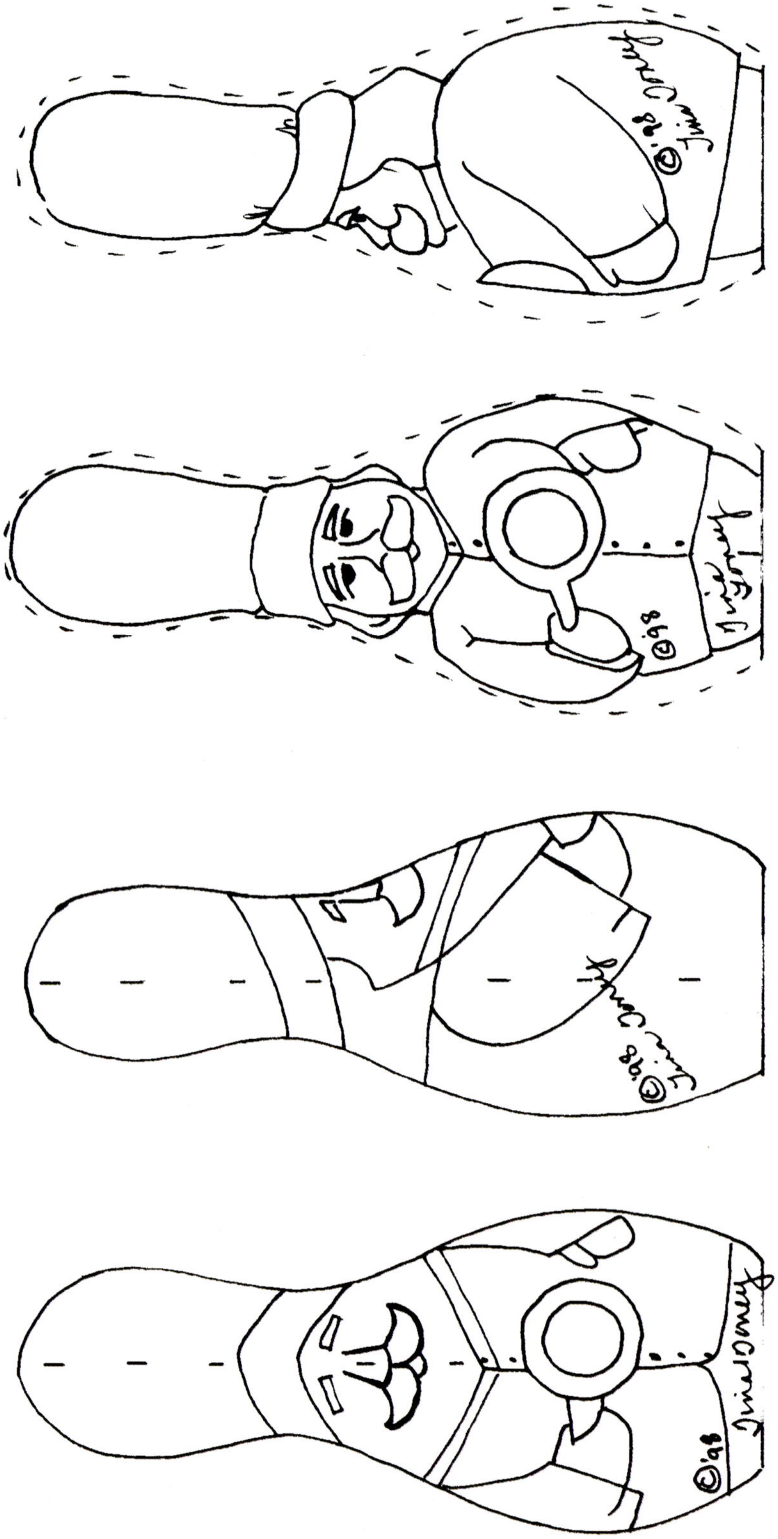

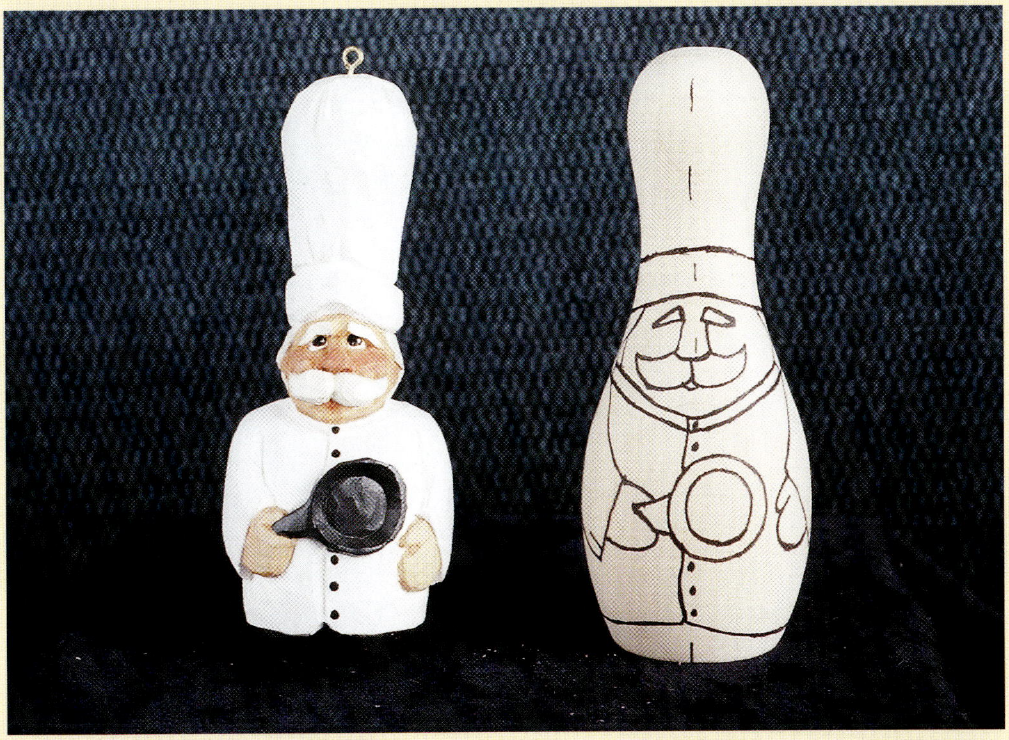

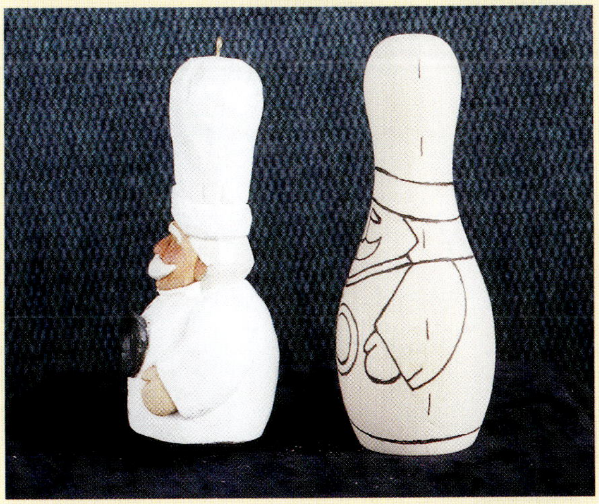

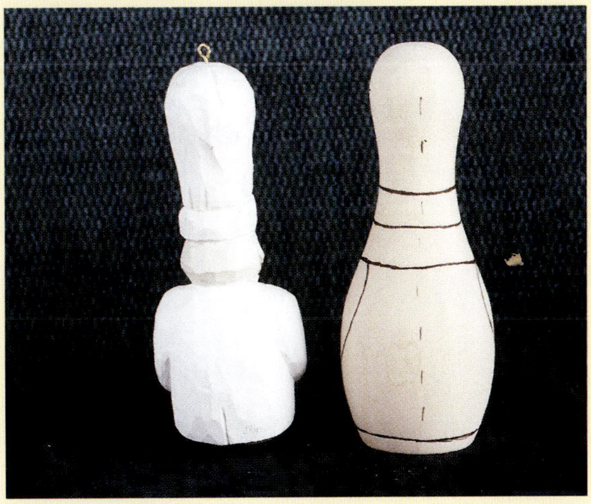

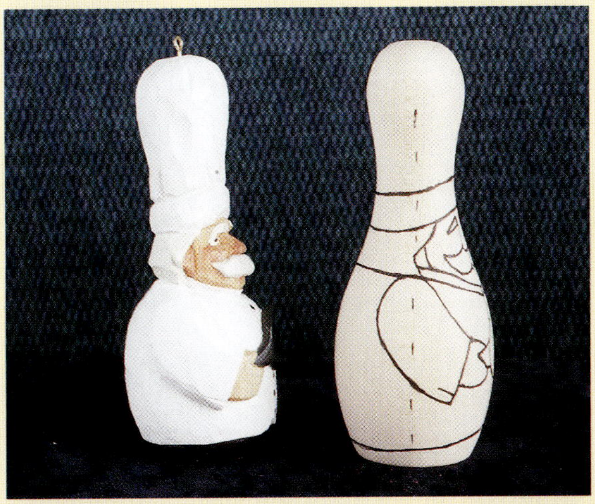

Bell Santa

Carved on Bell Shape Product #BTB-20

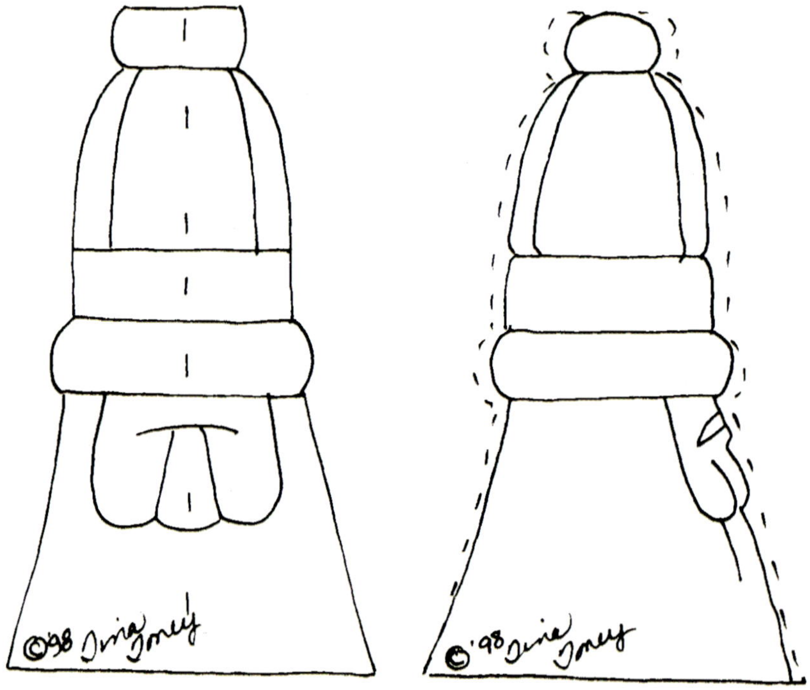

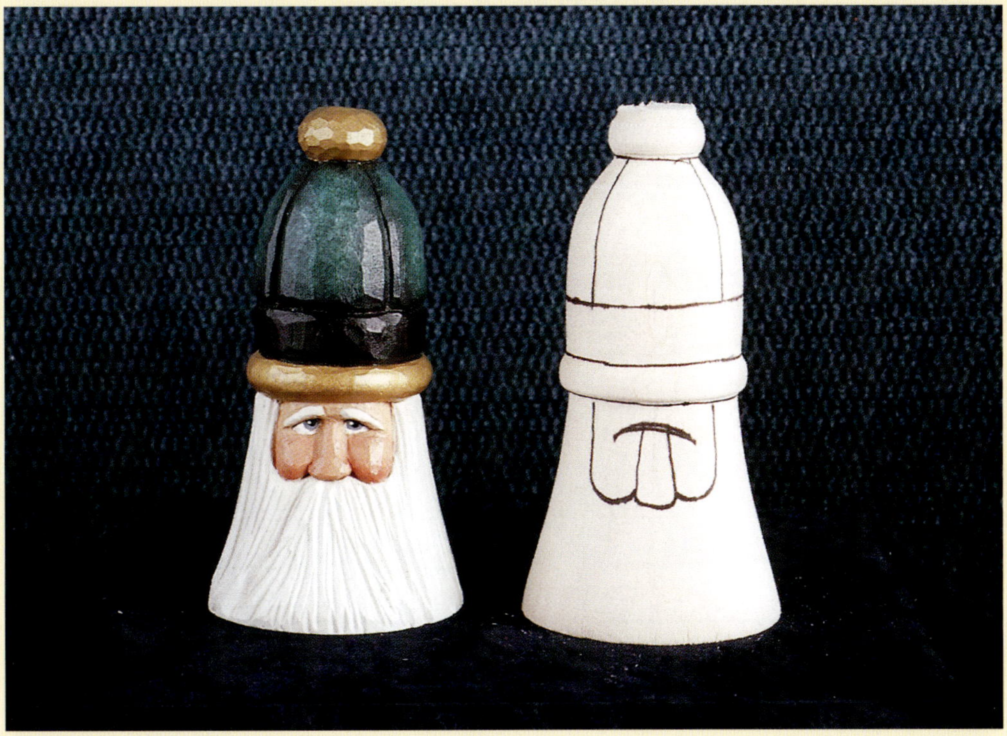

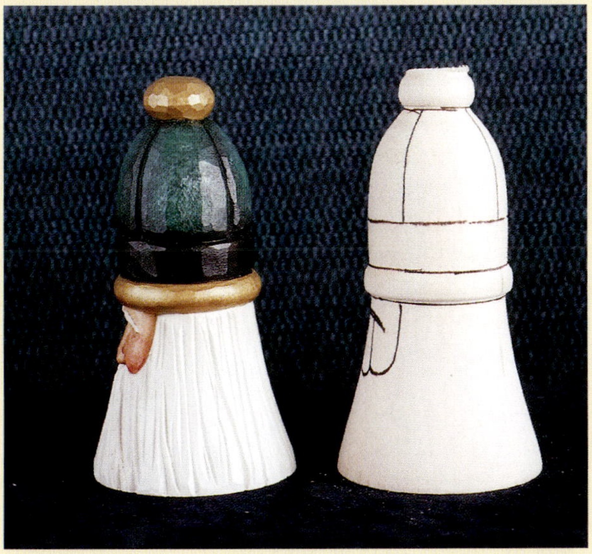

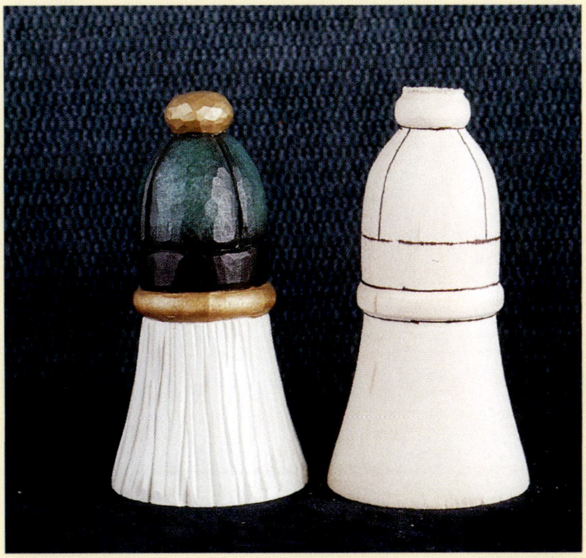

PÈRE NOËL

Carved on Footed Egg Product #TT-01

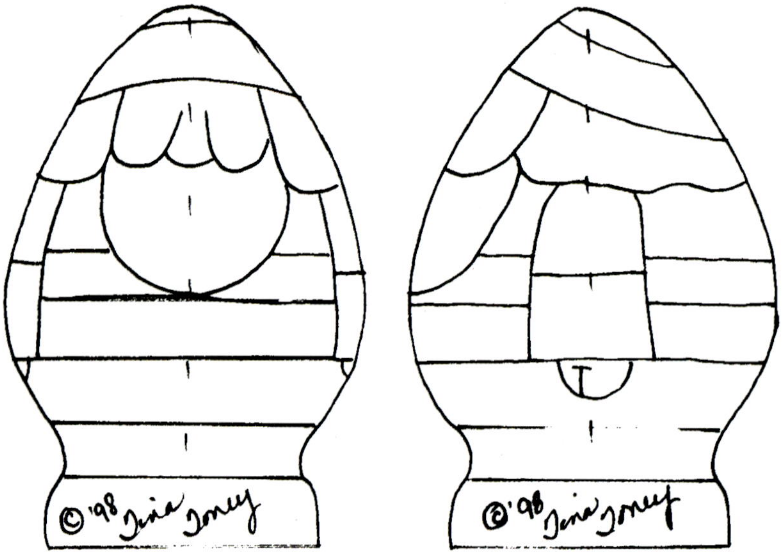

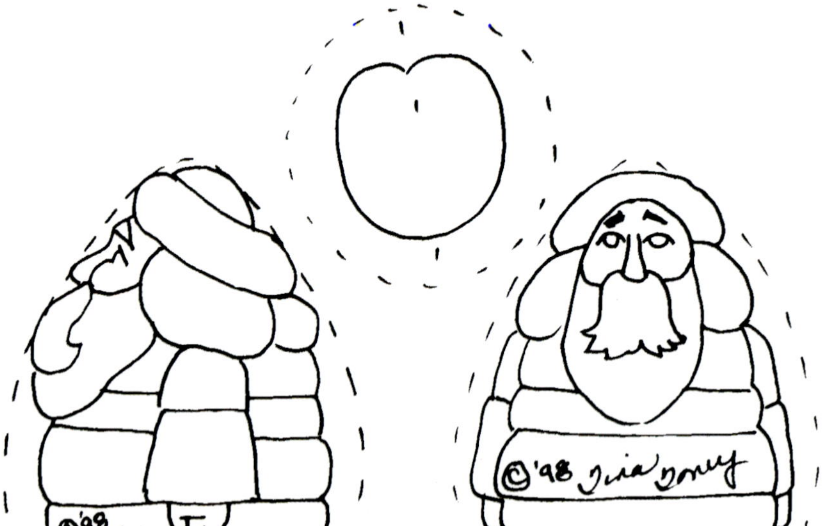

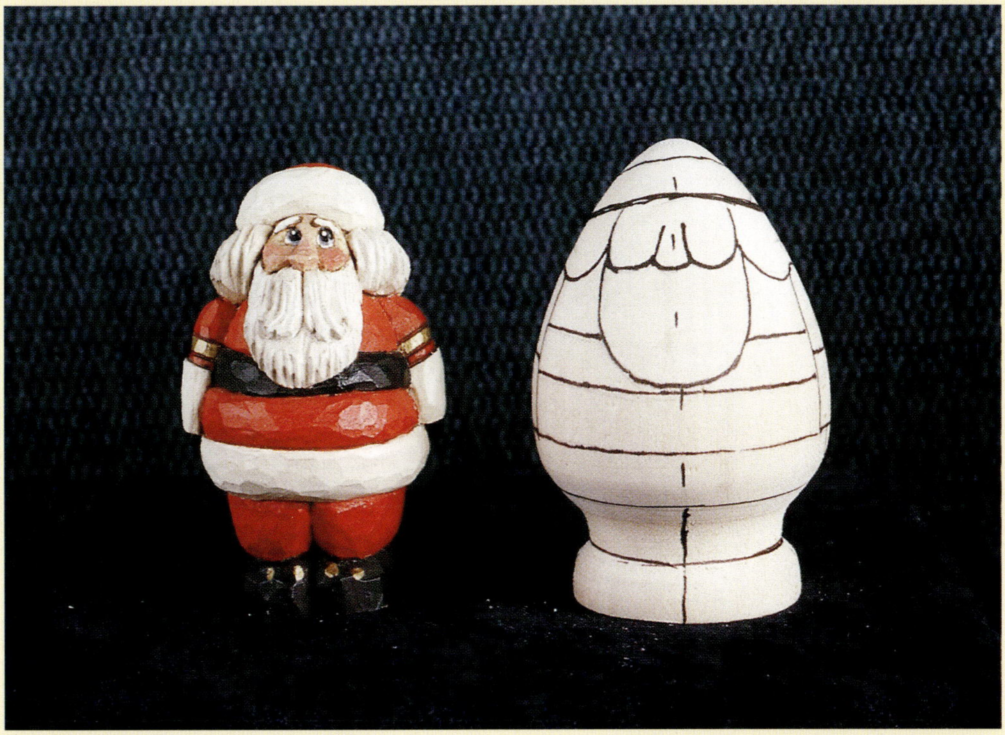

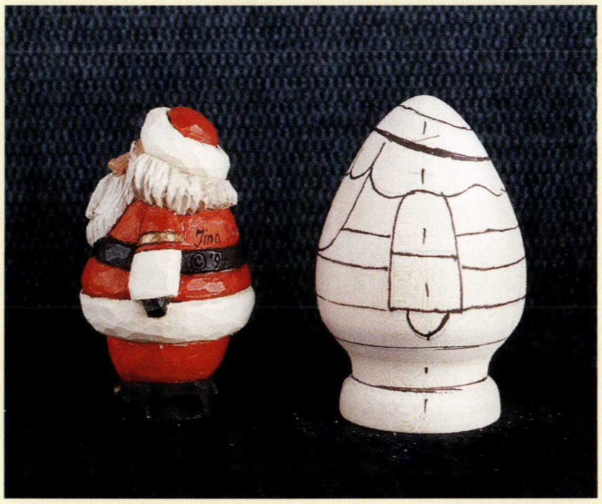

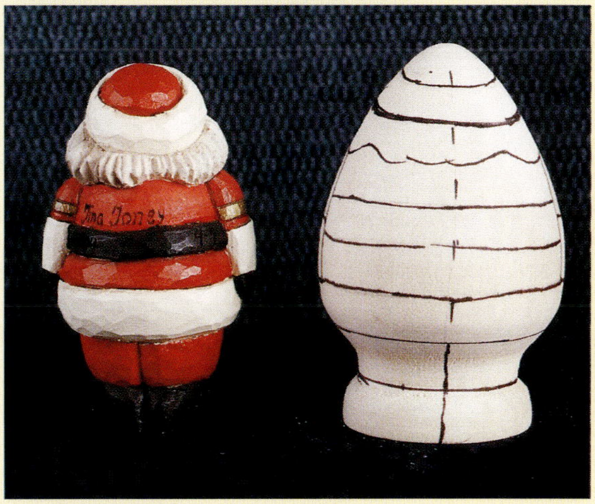

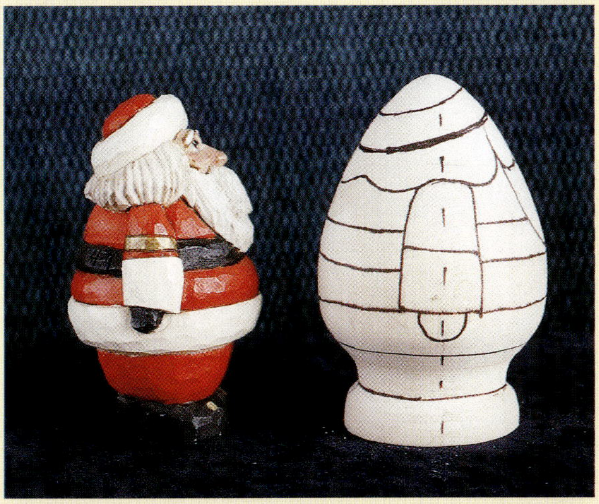

CHRISTKINDL

Carved on Mini-Roly-Poly Shape #BTS-011S

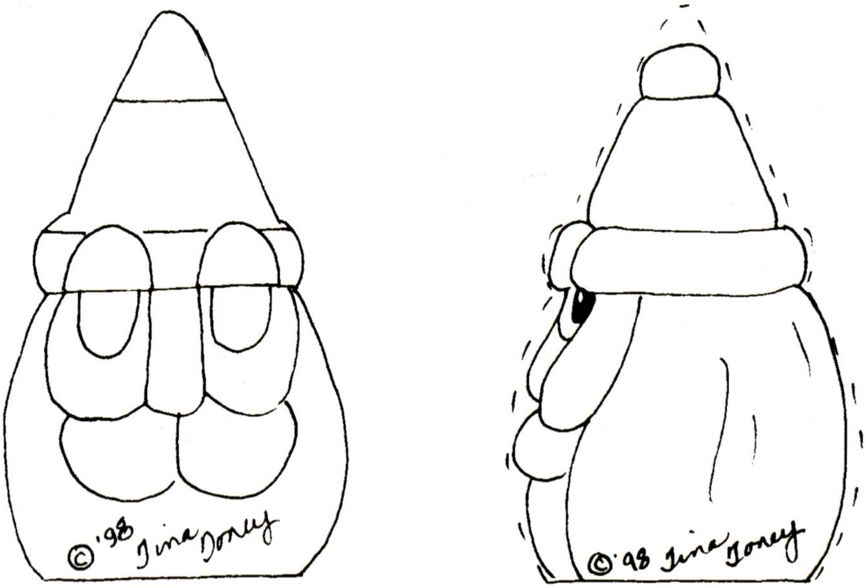

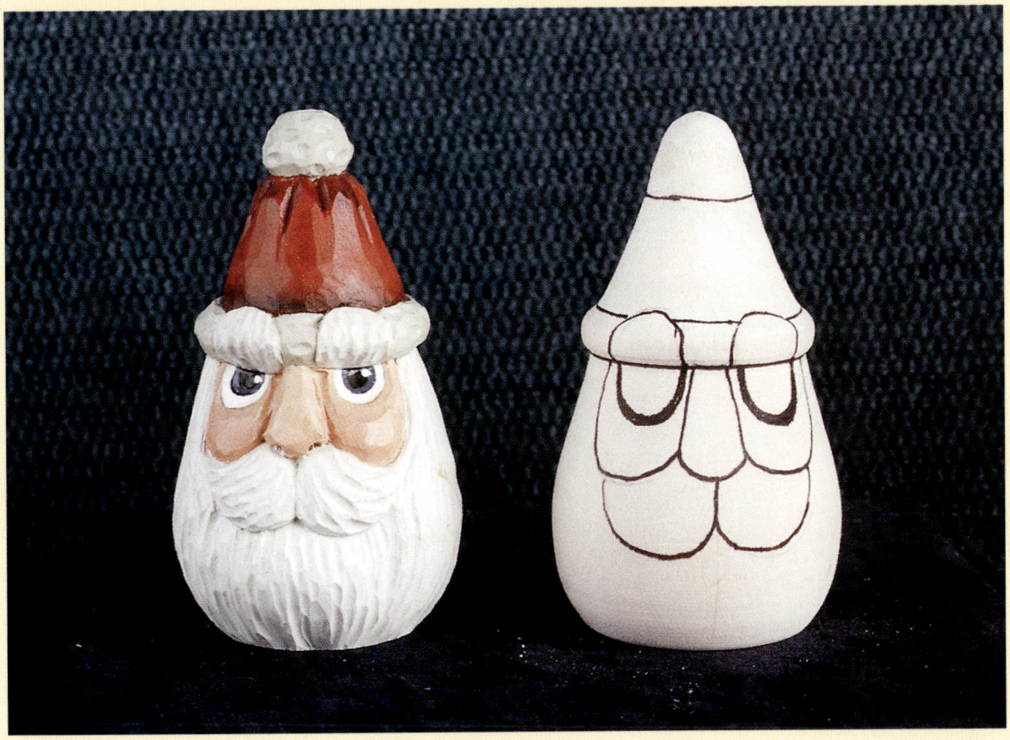

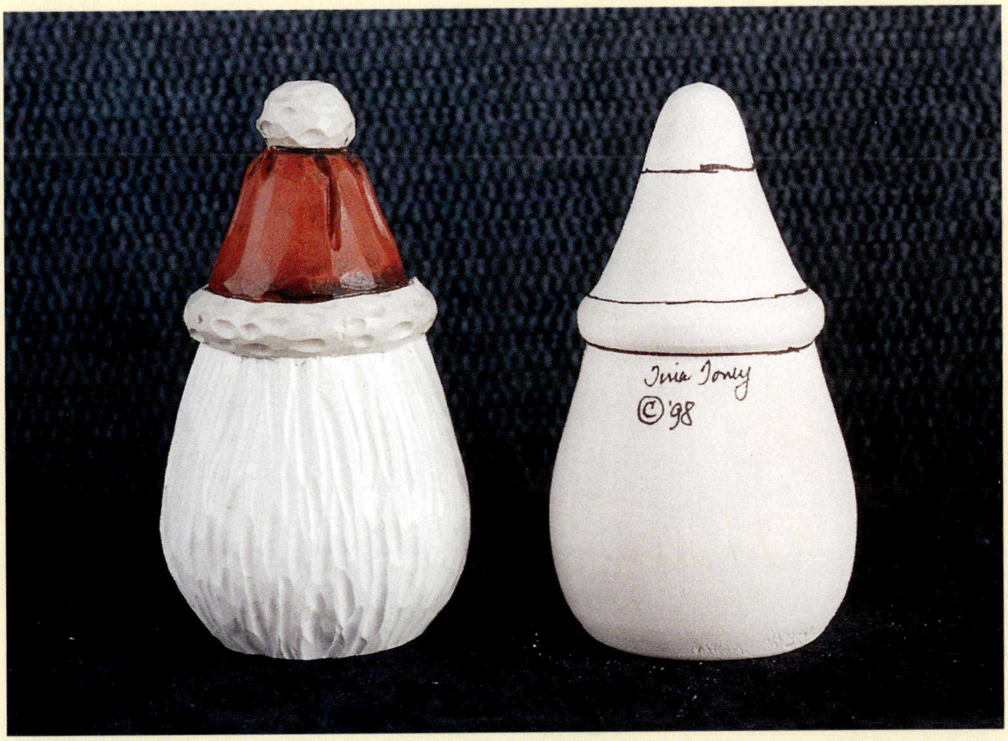
Iris Toney
©'98

THE CHRISTMAS GNOME

Carved on Gnome Shape Product #BTE-01

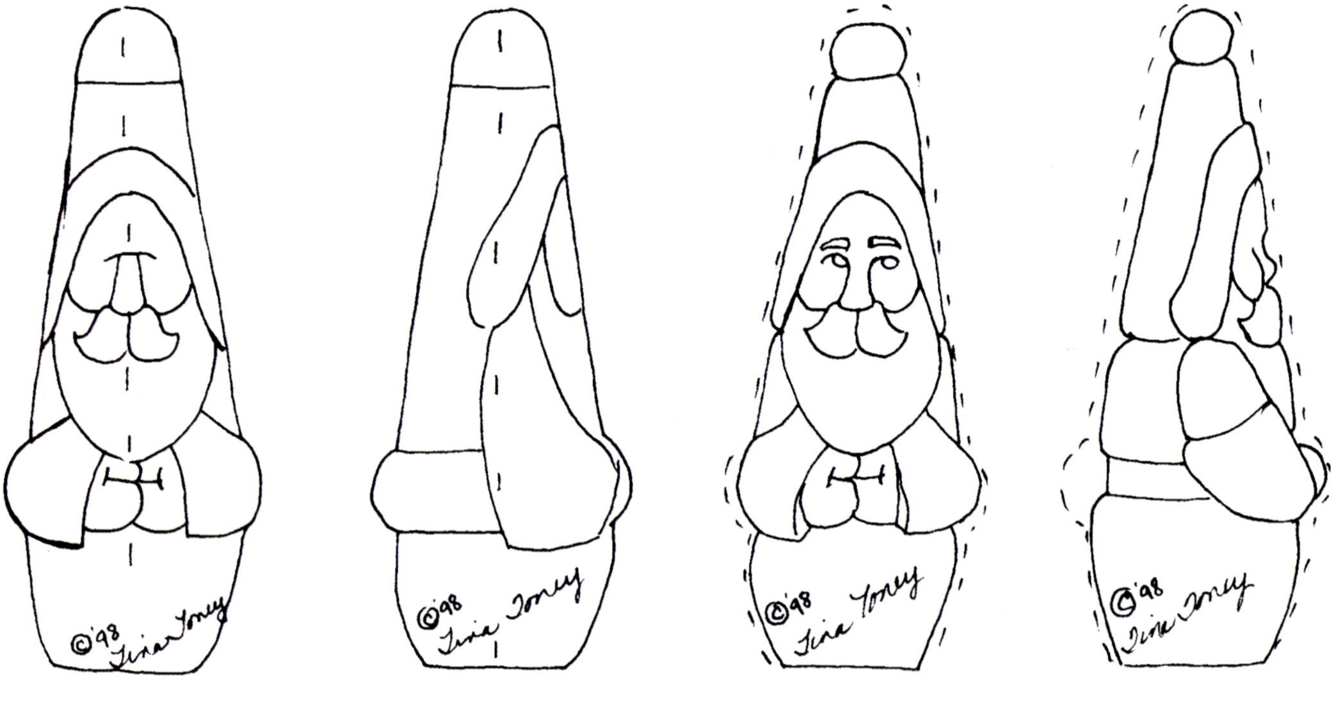

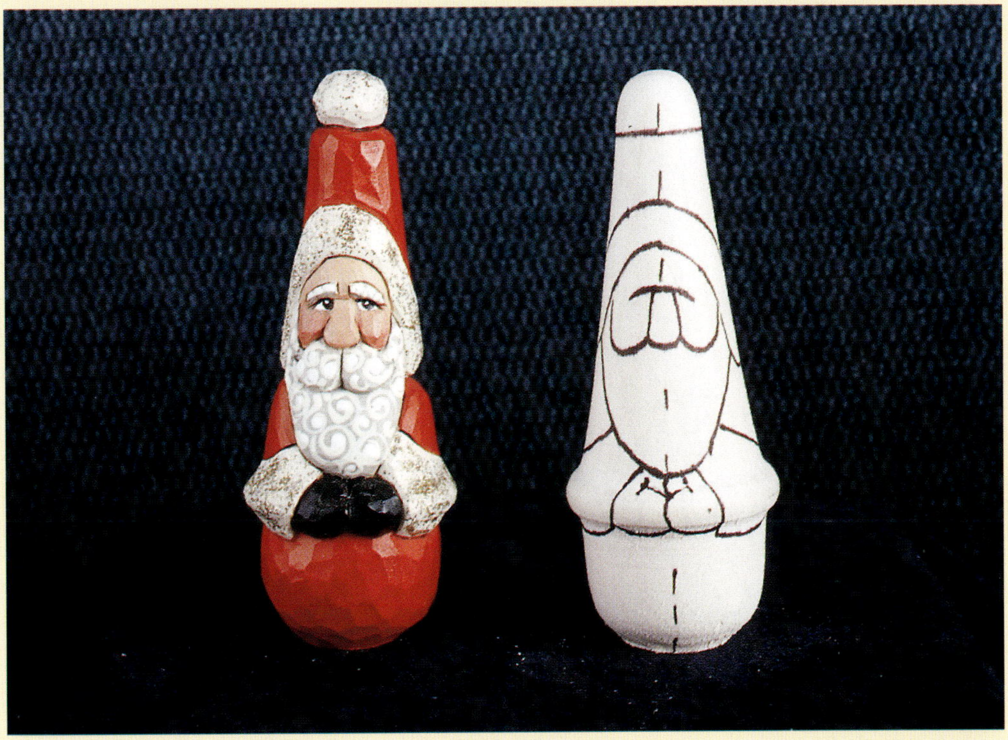

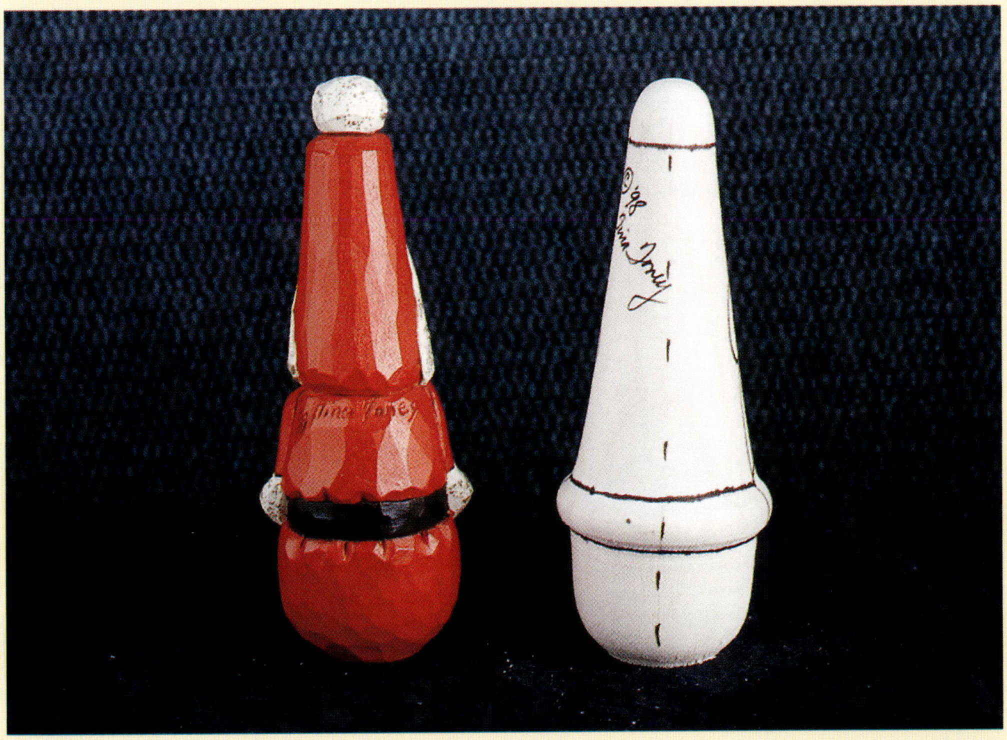

LONGBEARD

Carved on Product #BTFO-01

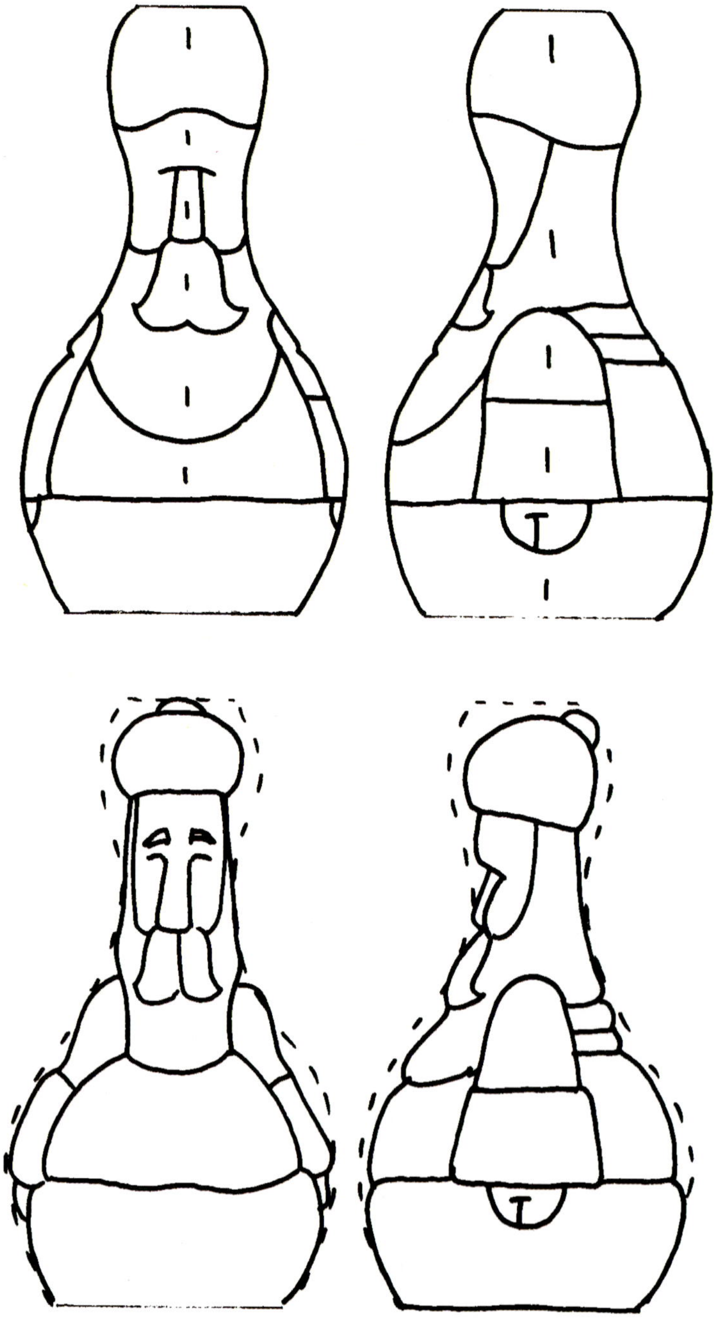

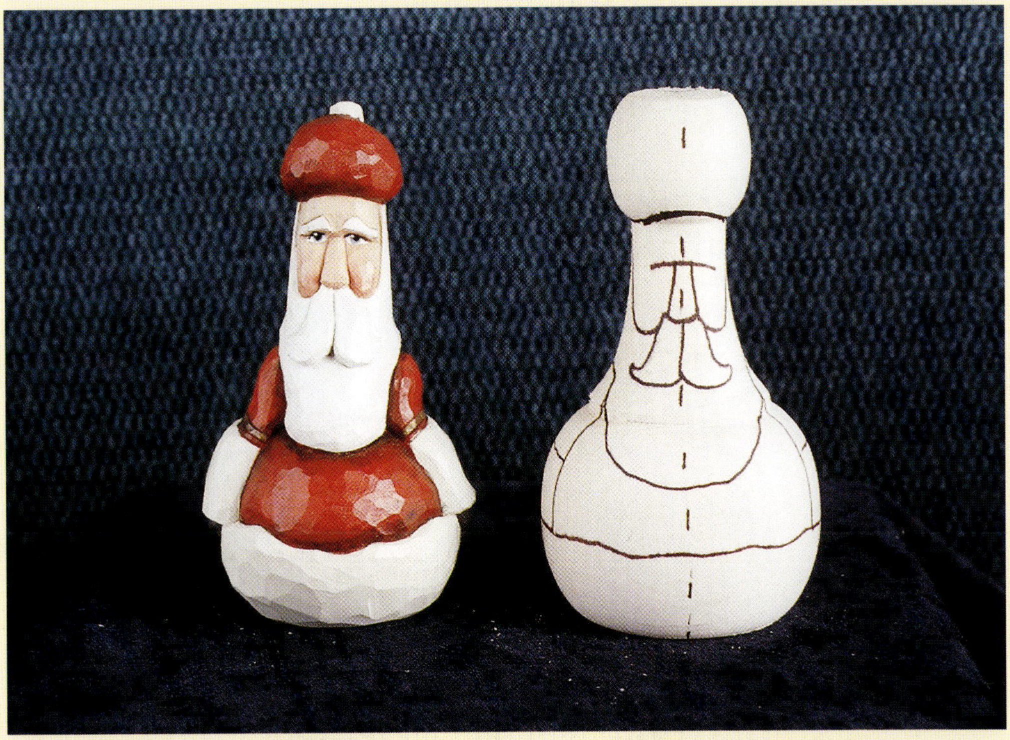

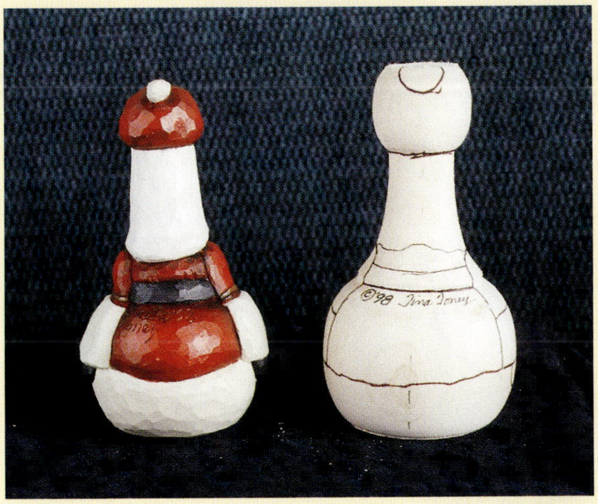

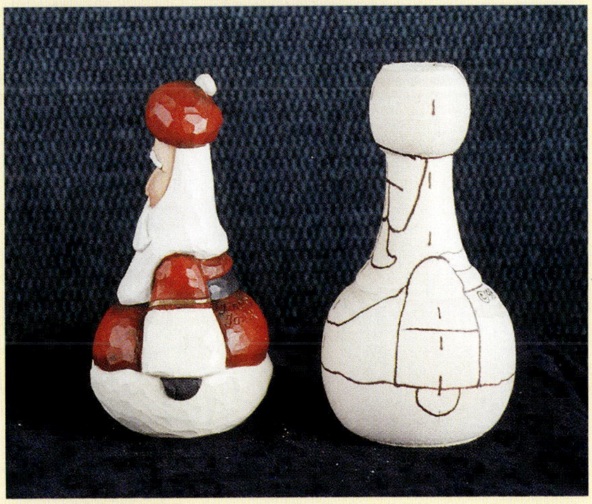

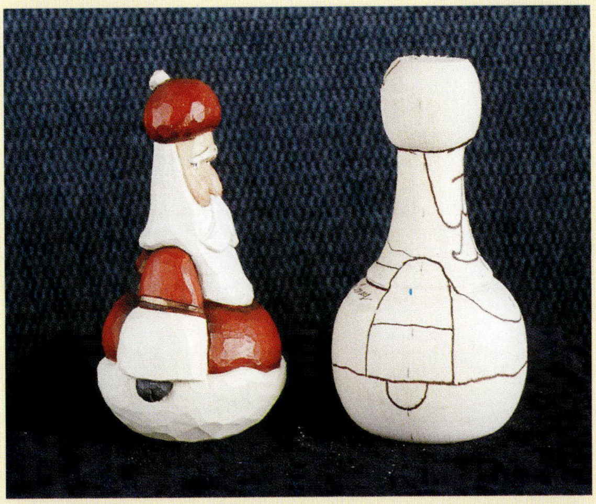

Niklaus

Carved on Bell Shape Product #BTB-20

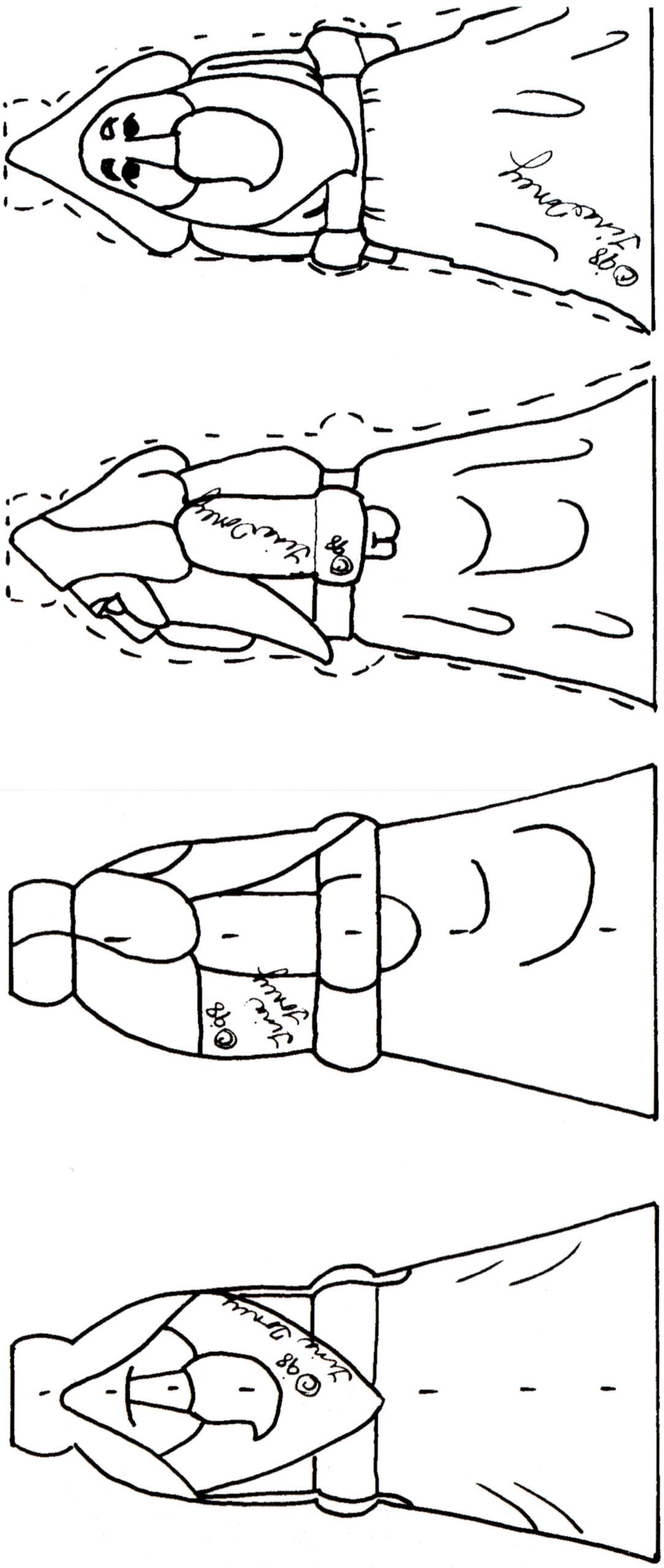

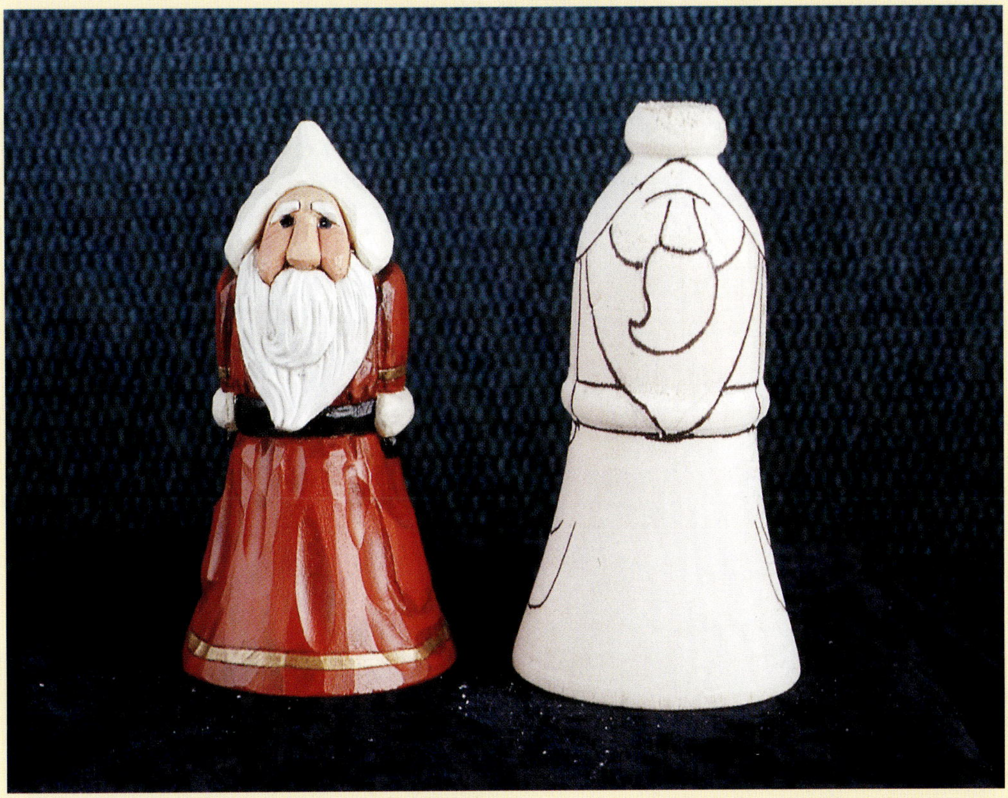

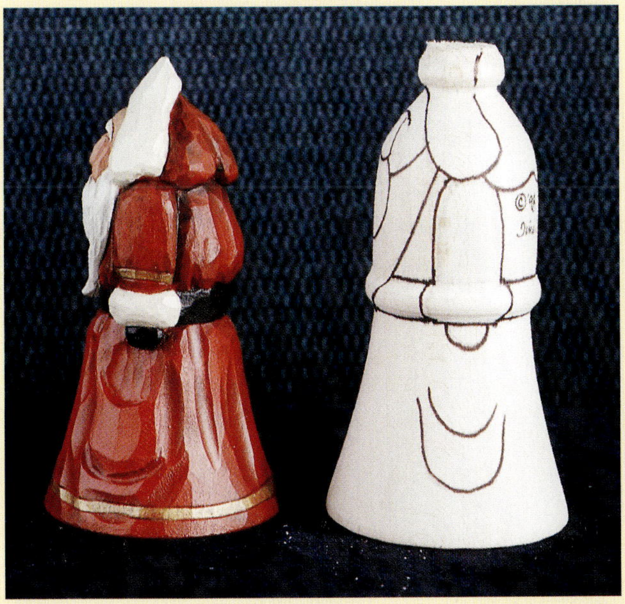

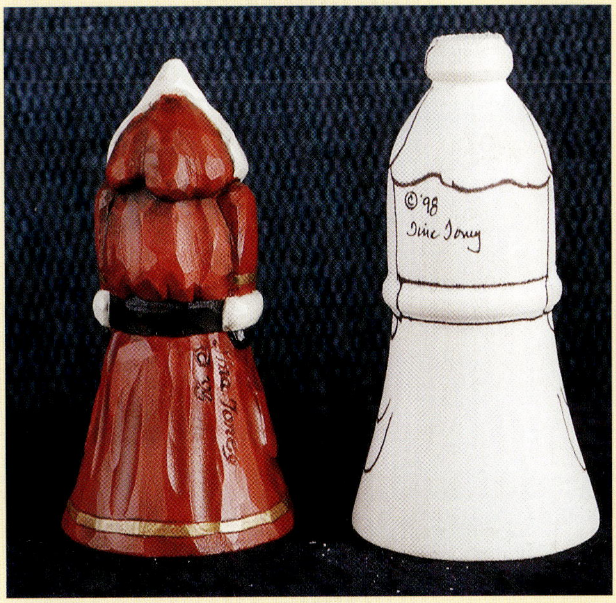

PRIMITIVE SANTA

Carved on Ornament Shape #SBTO-01

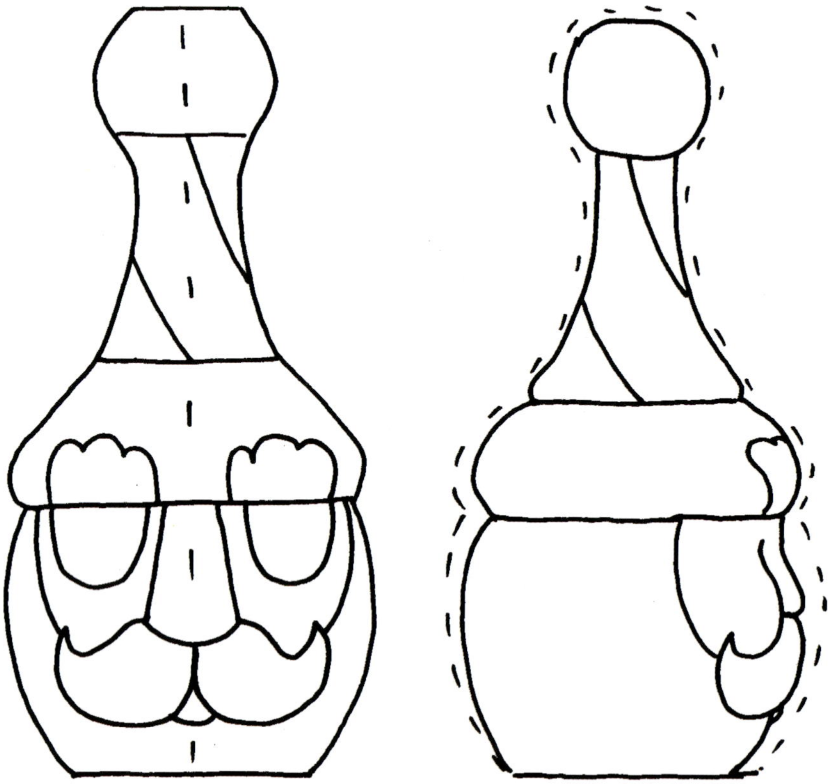

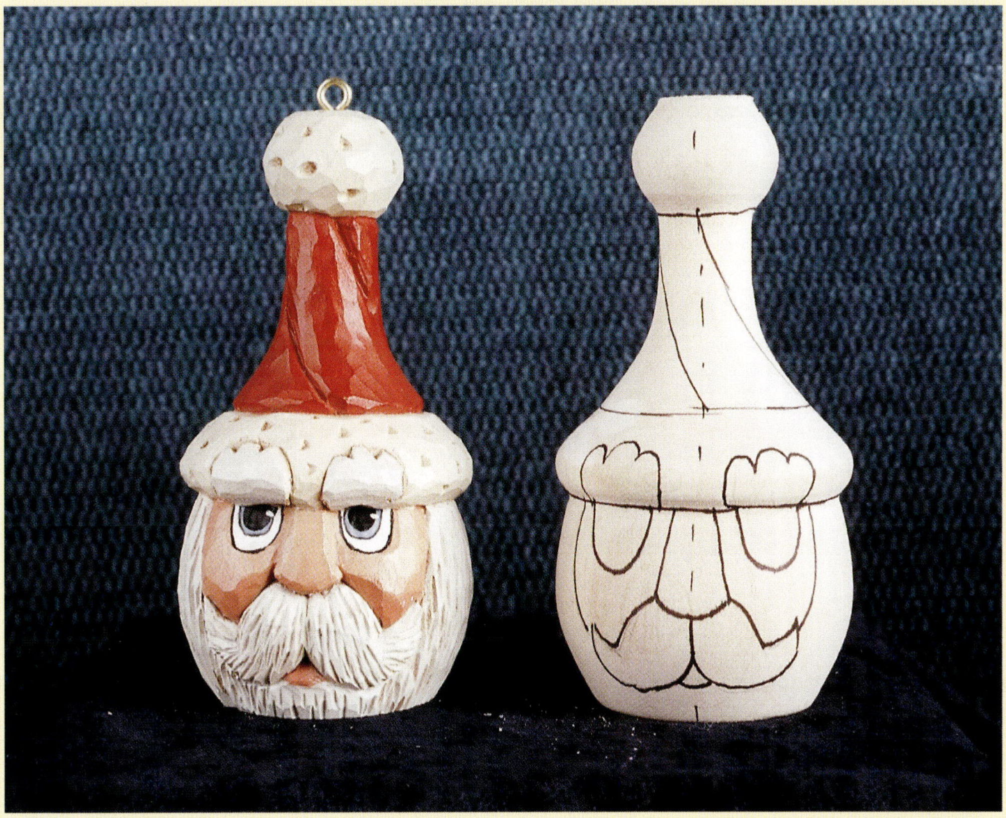

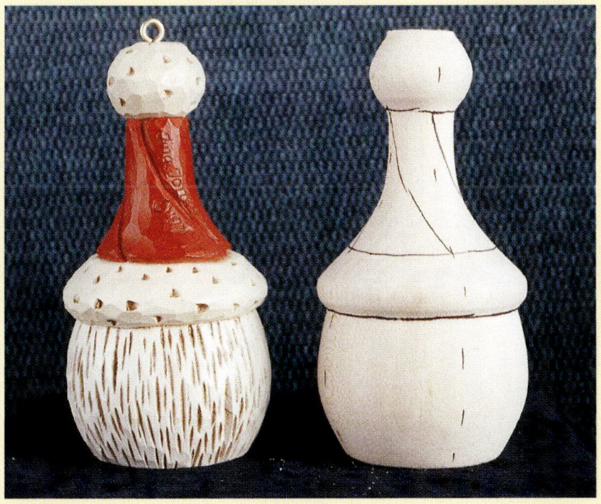

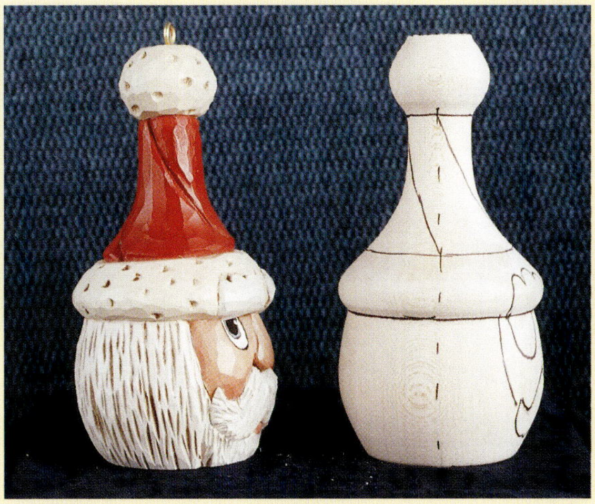

THE BUSINESSMAN

Carved on Mini-Roly-Poly Product #BTS-011S

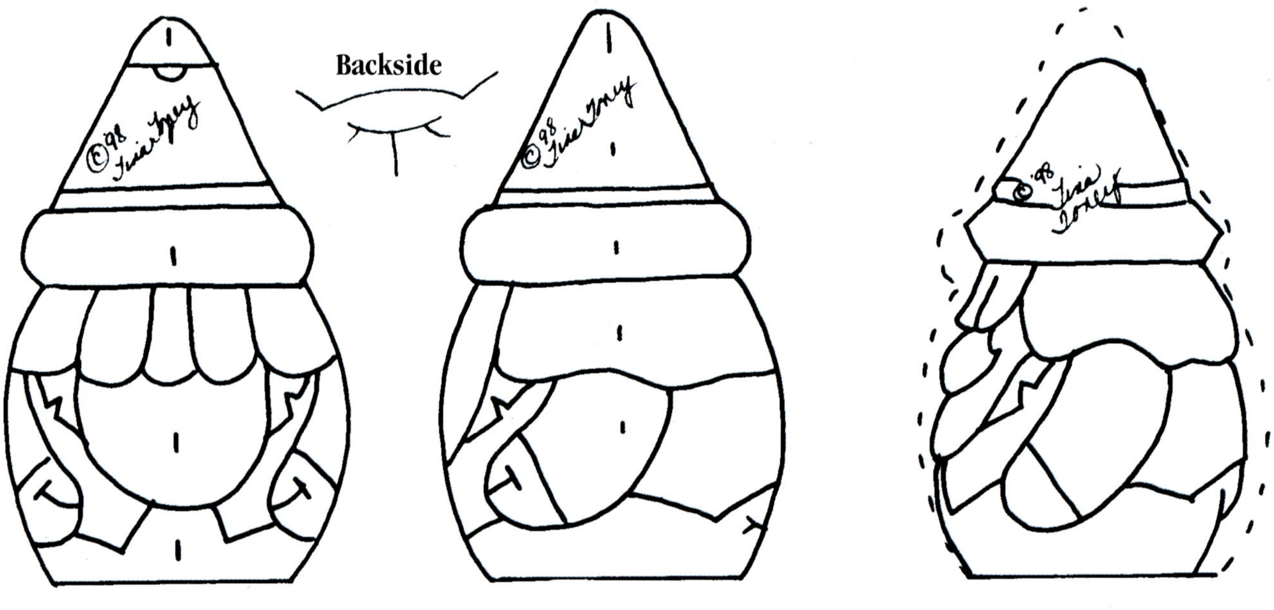

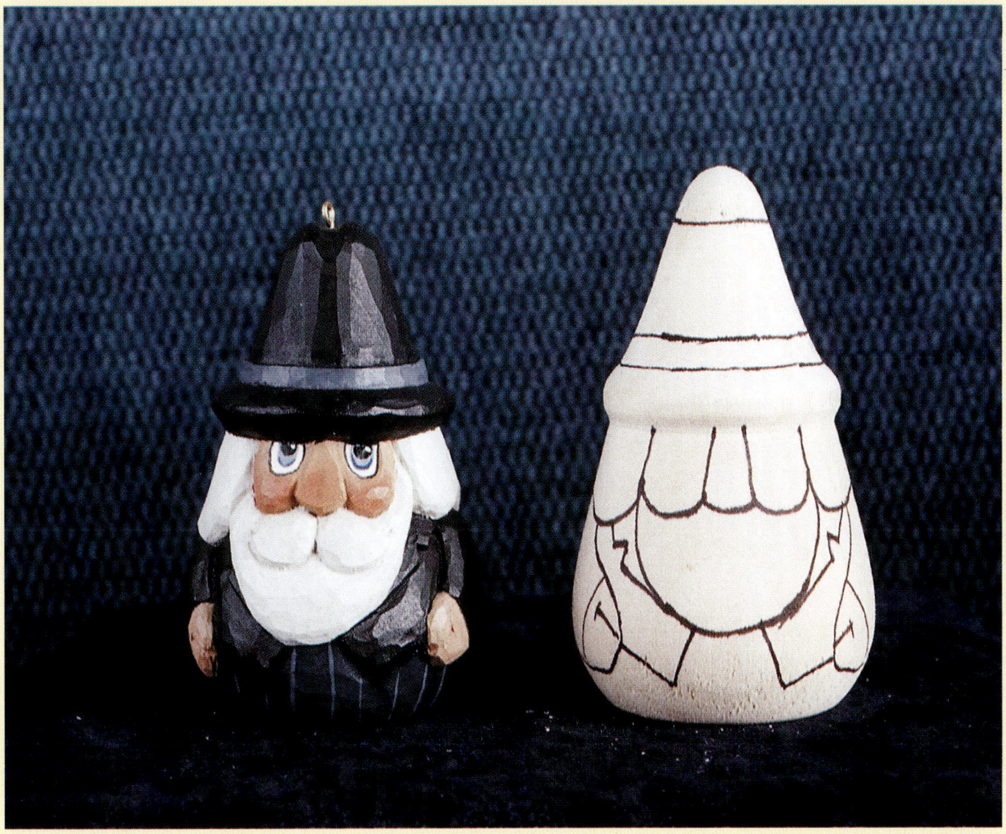

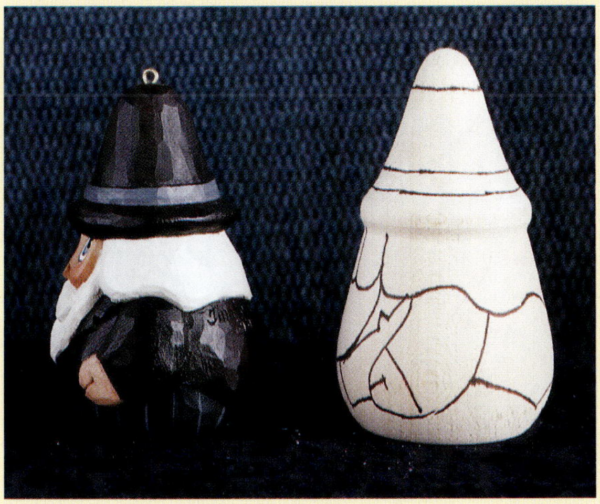

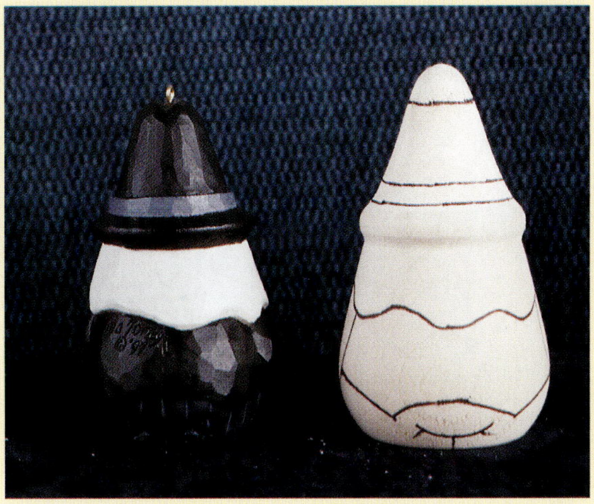

BALDY SANTA

Carved on Goose Egg Product #BTEG

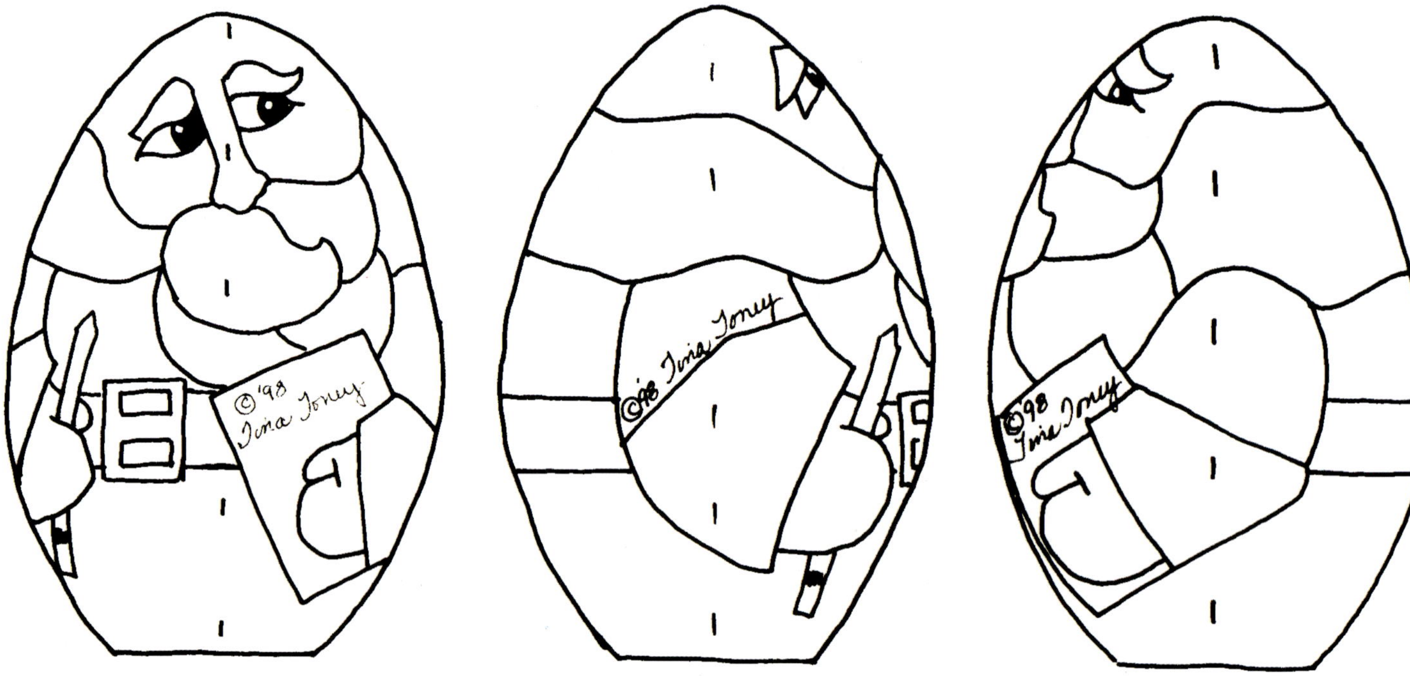

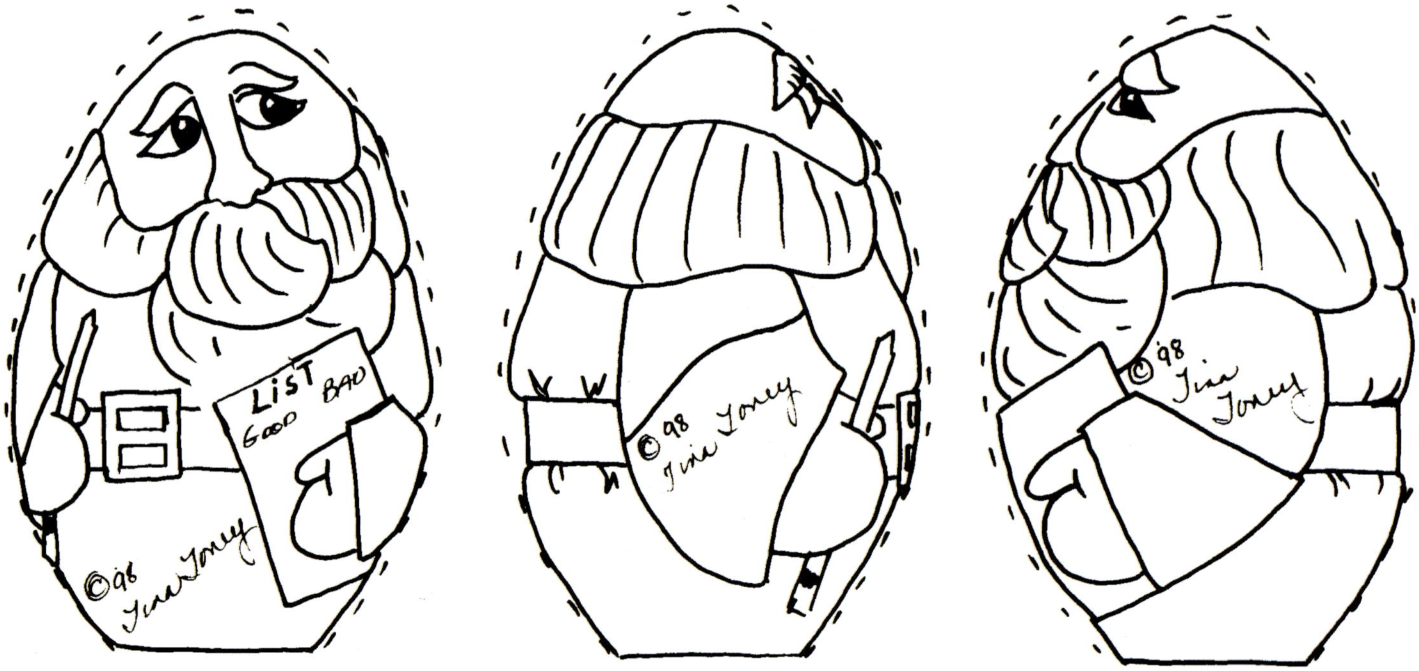

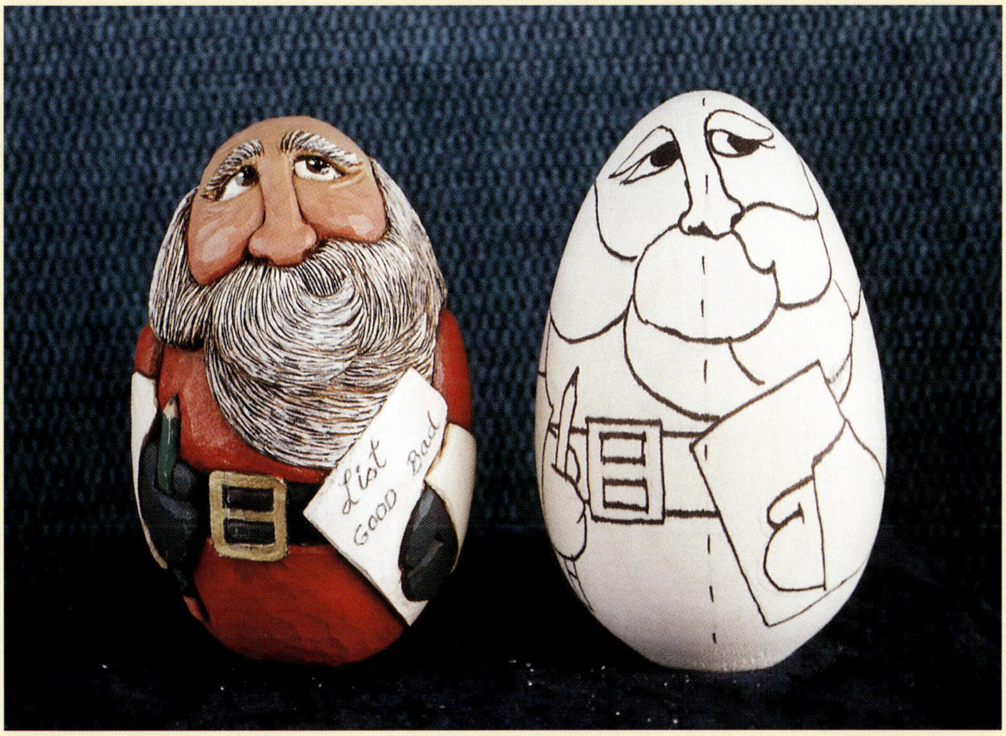
List
GOOD Bad

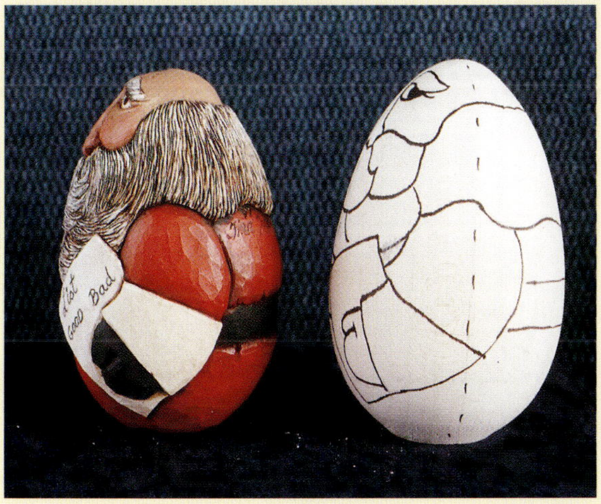
List
GOOD Bad

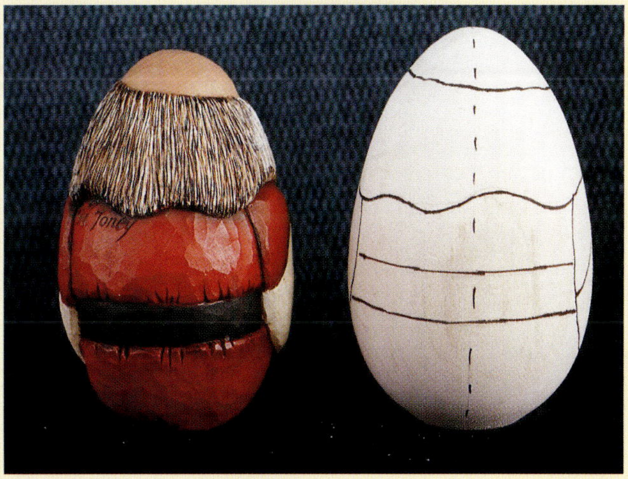

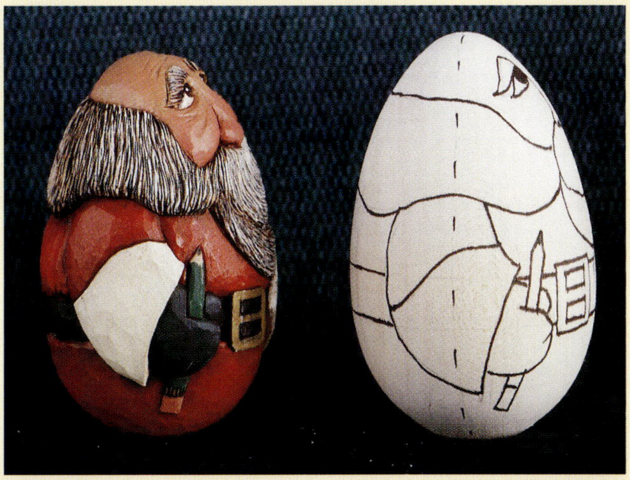

THE ELFIN SANTA

Carved on Gnome Shape Product #BTE-01

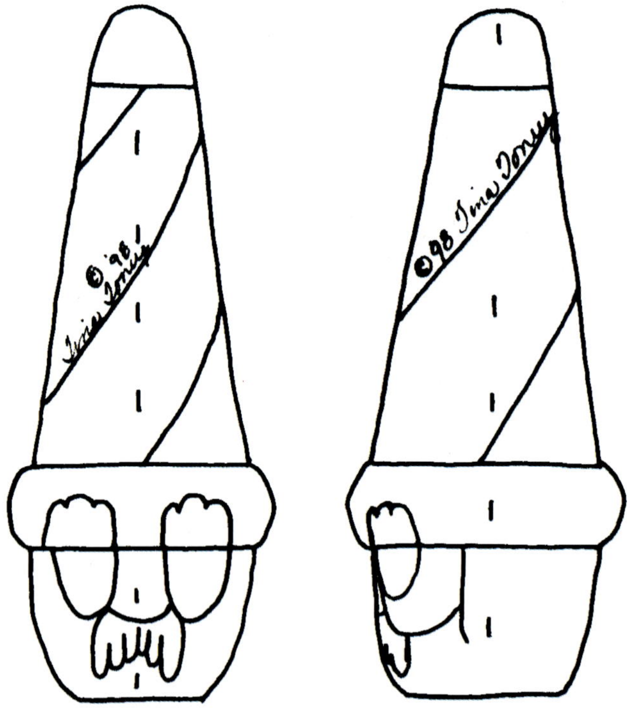

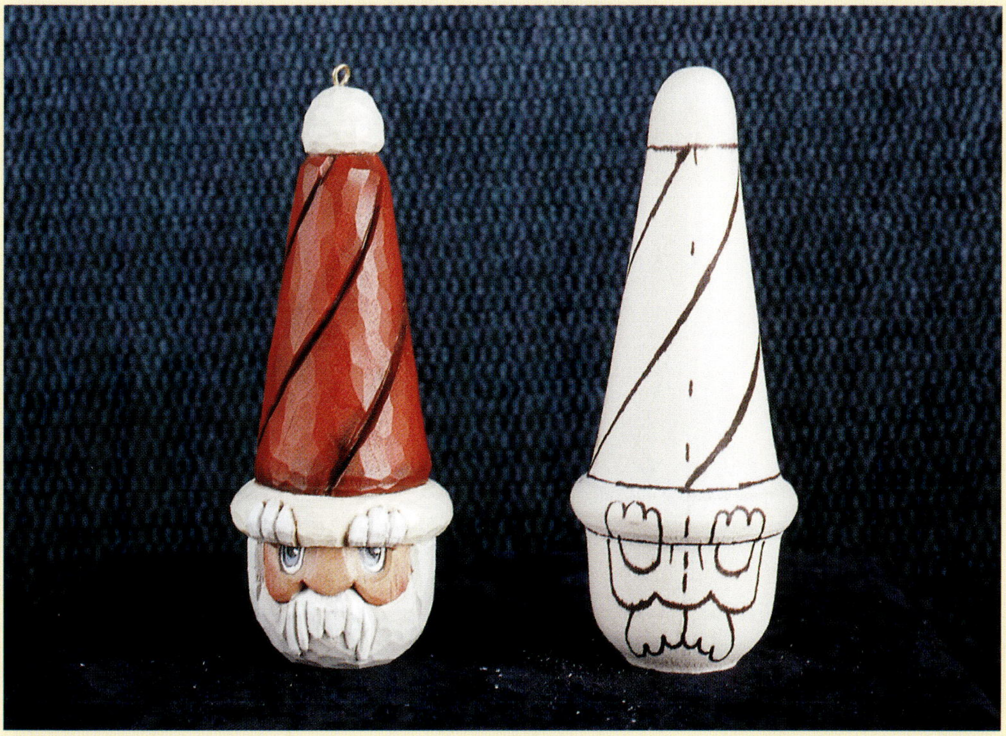

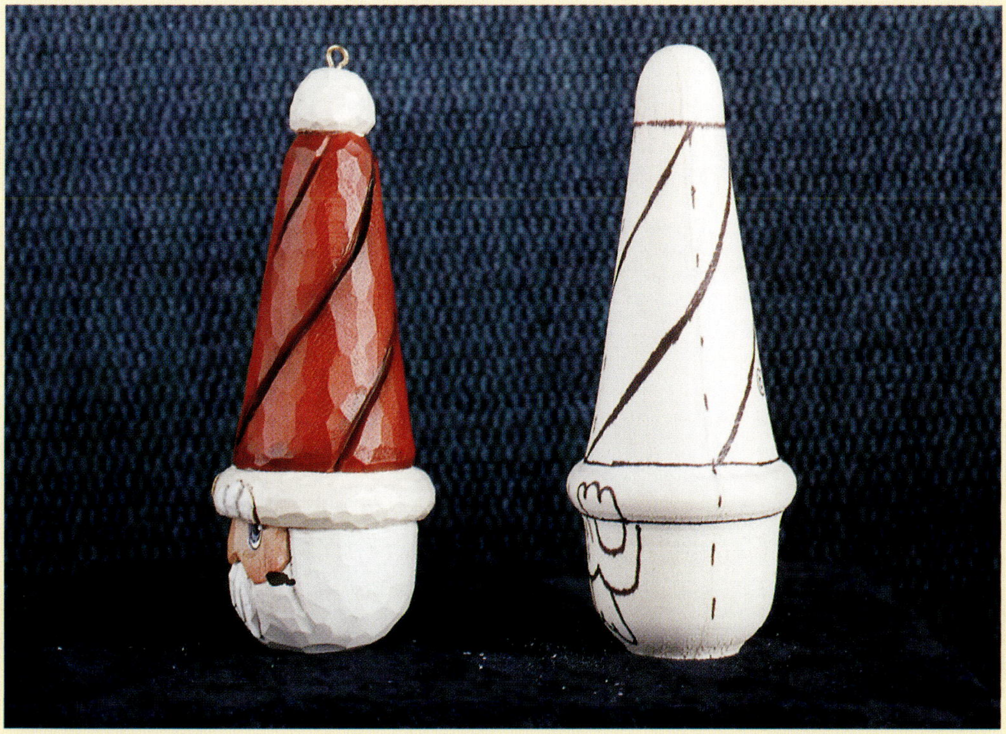

APPLE SANTA

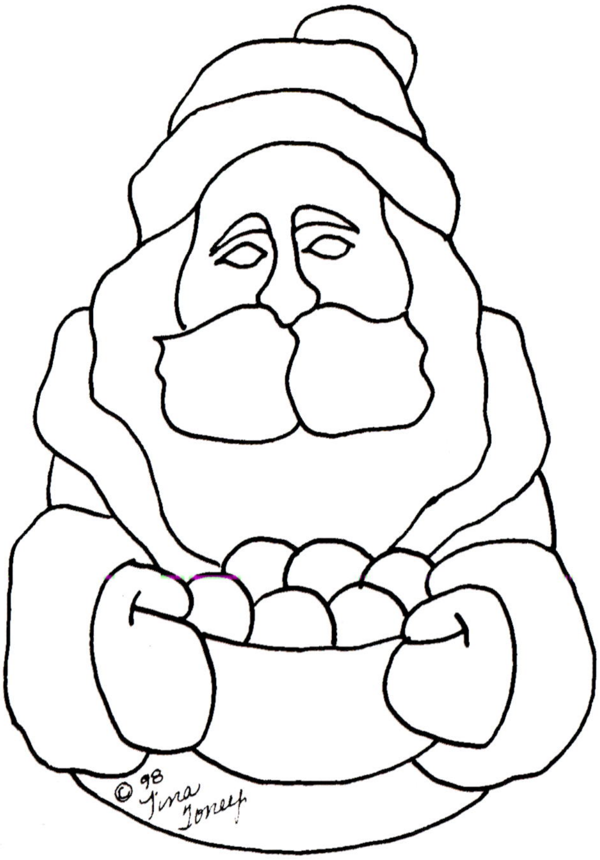

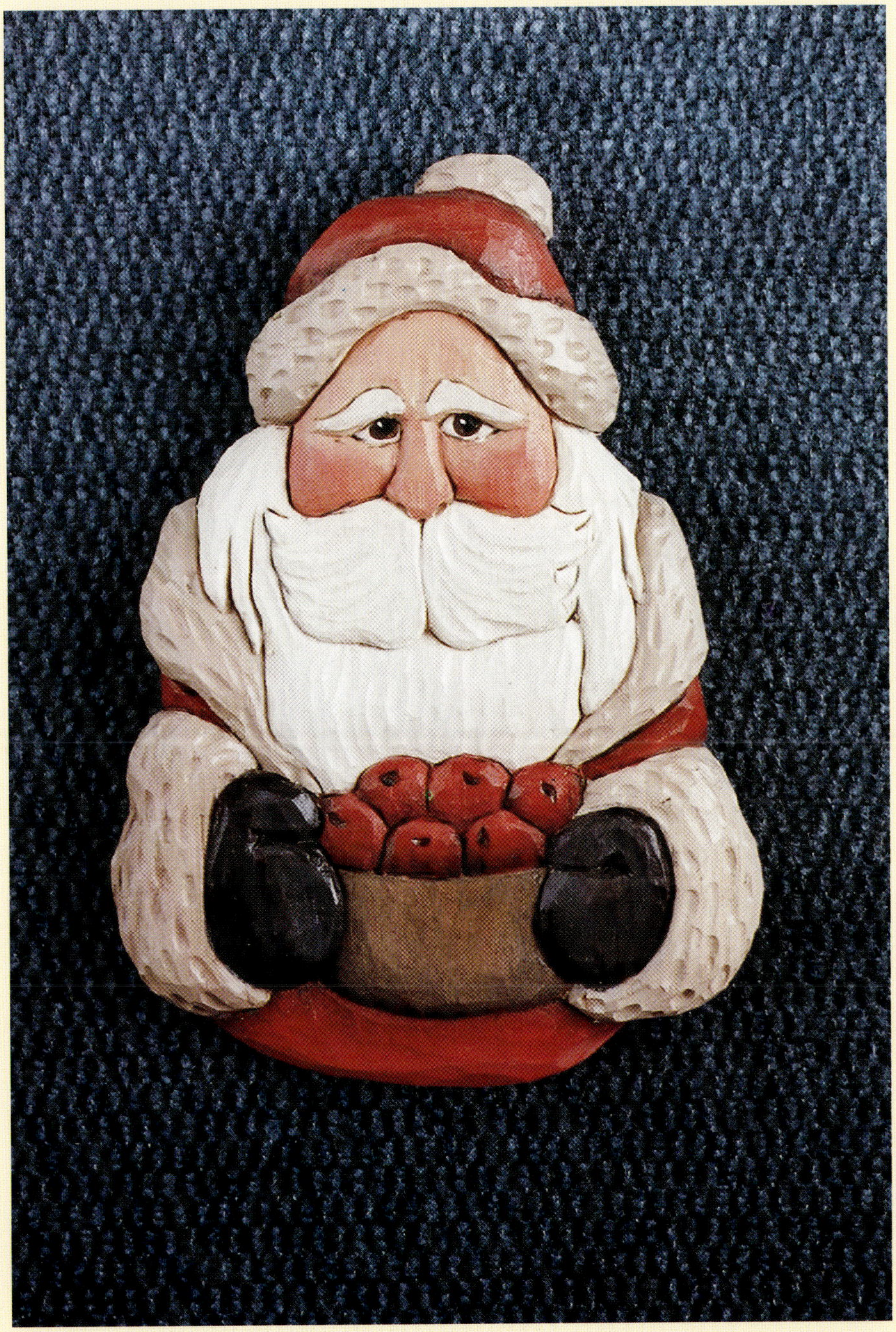

CHUBBY SANTA

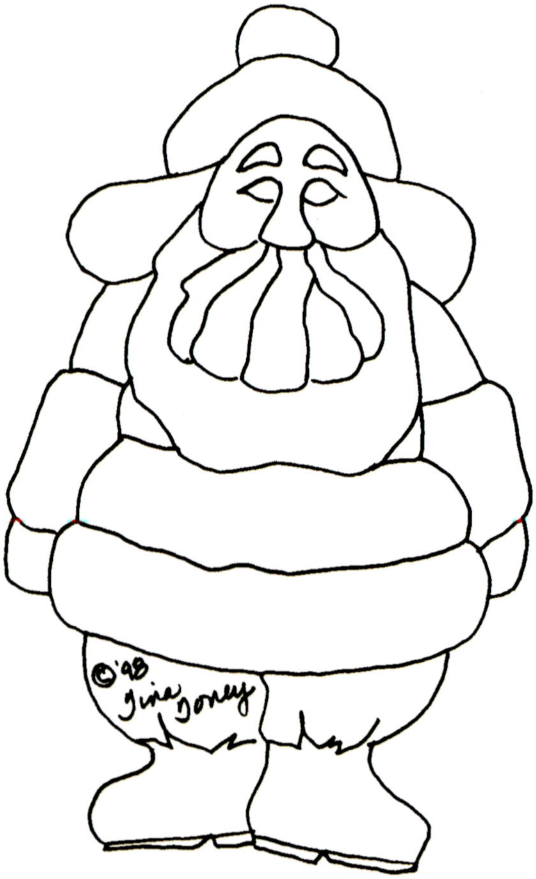

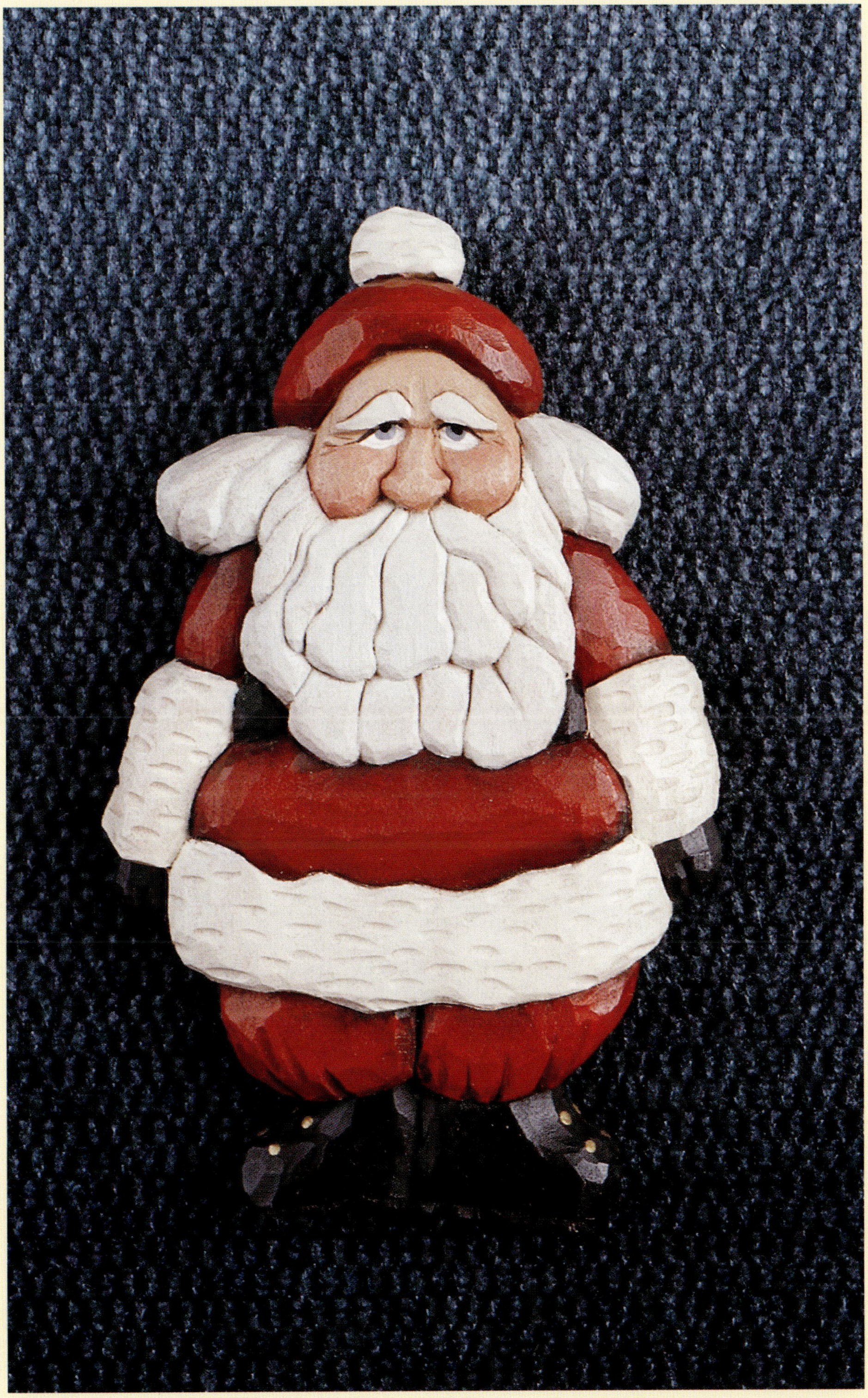

HAPPY SNOWMAN

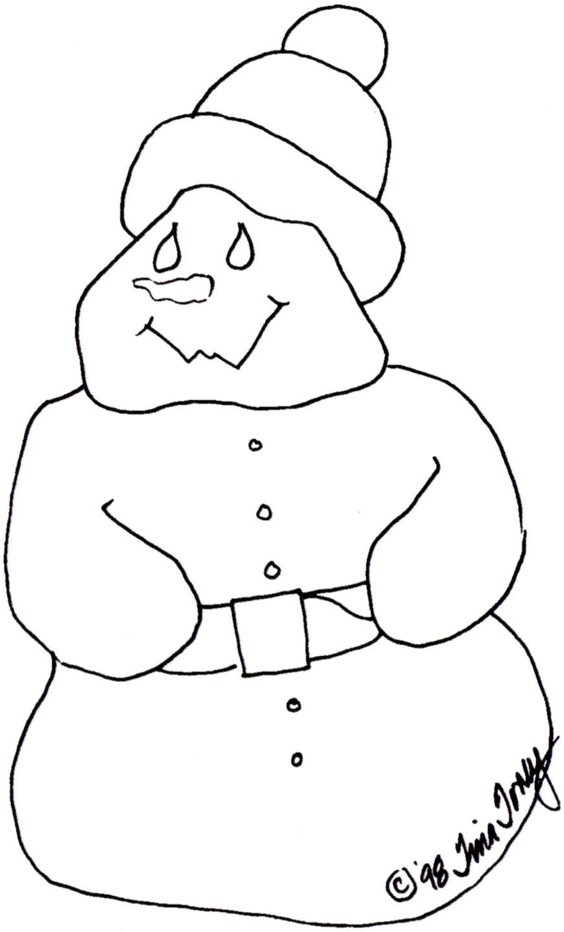

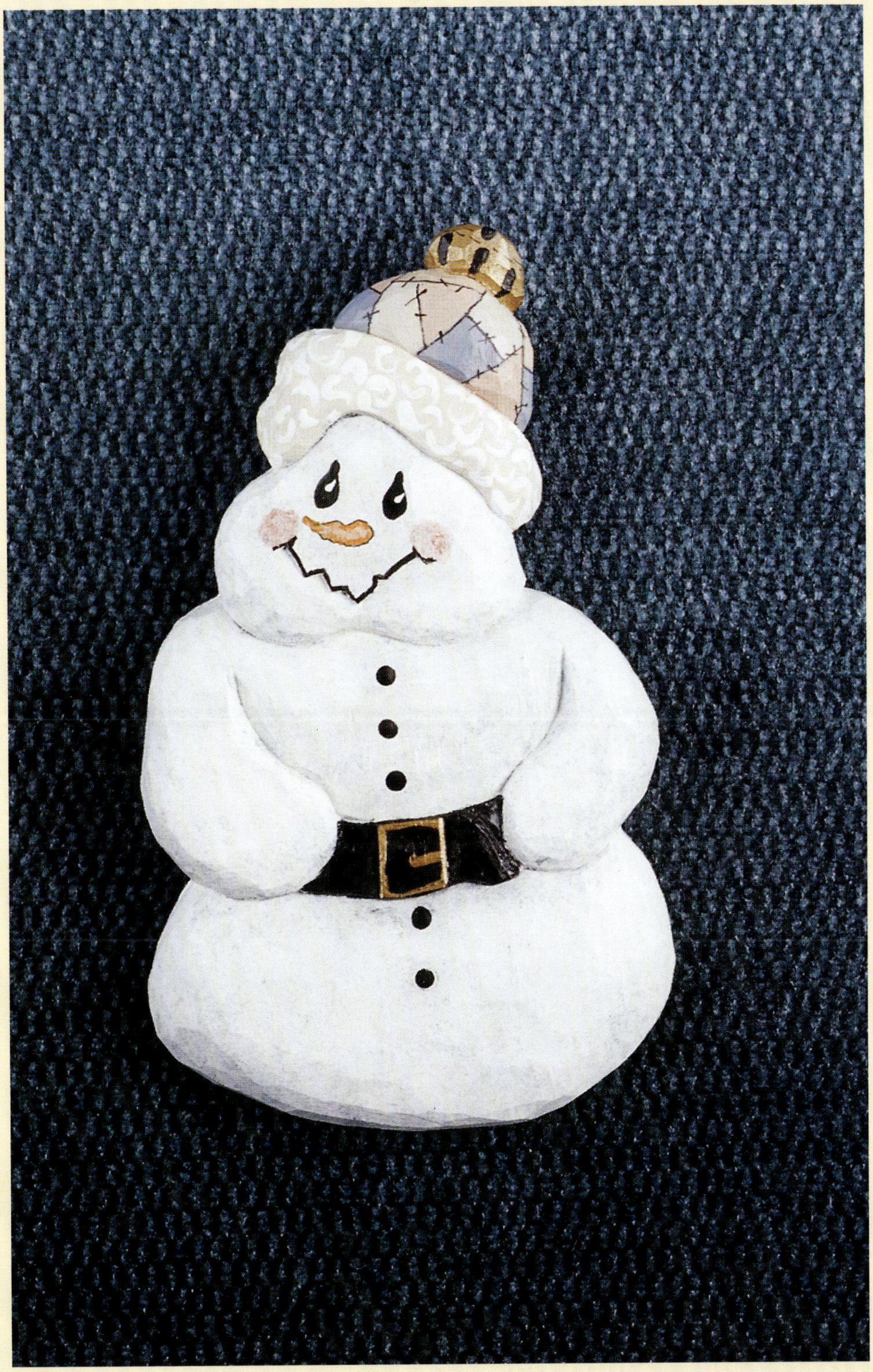

SANTA WITH TIPPED HAT

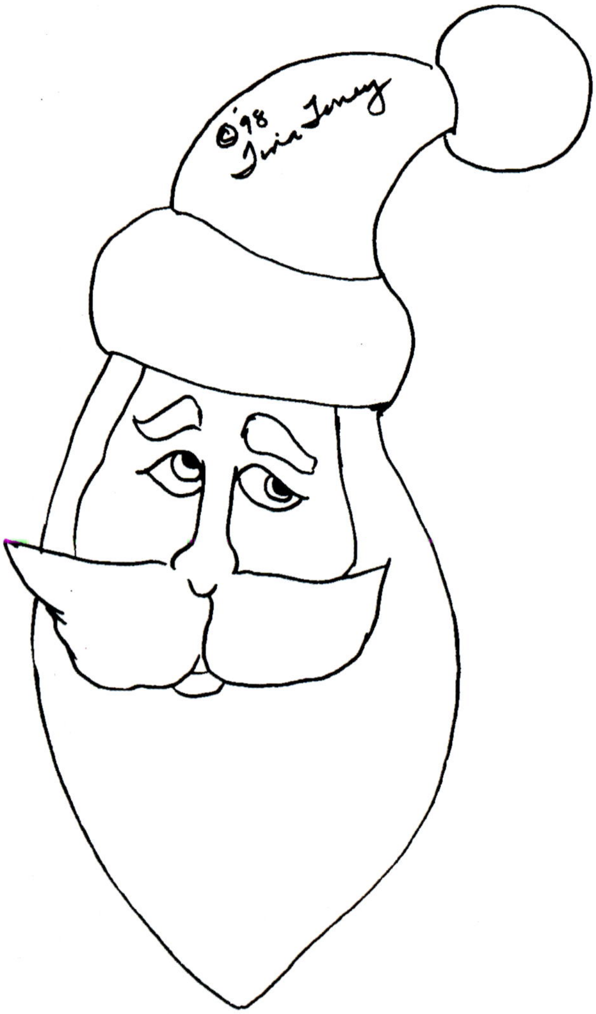

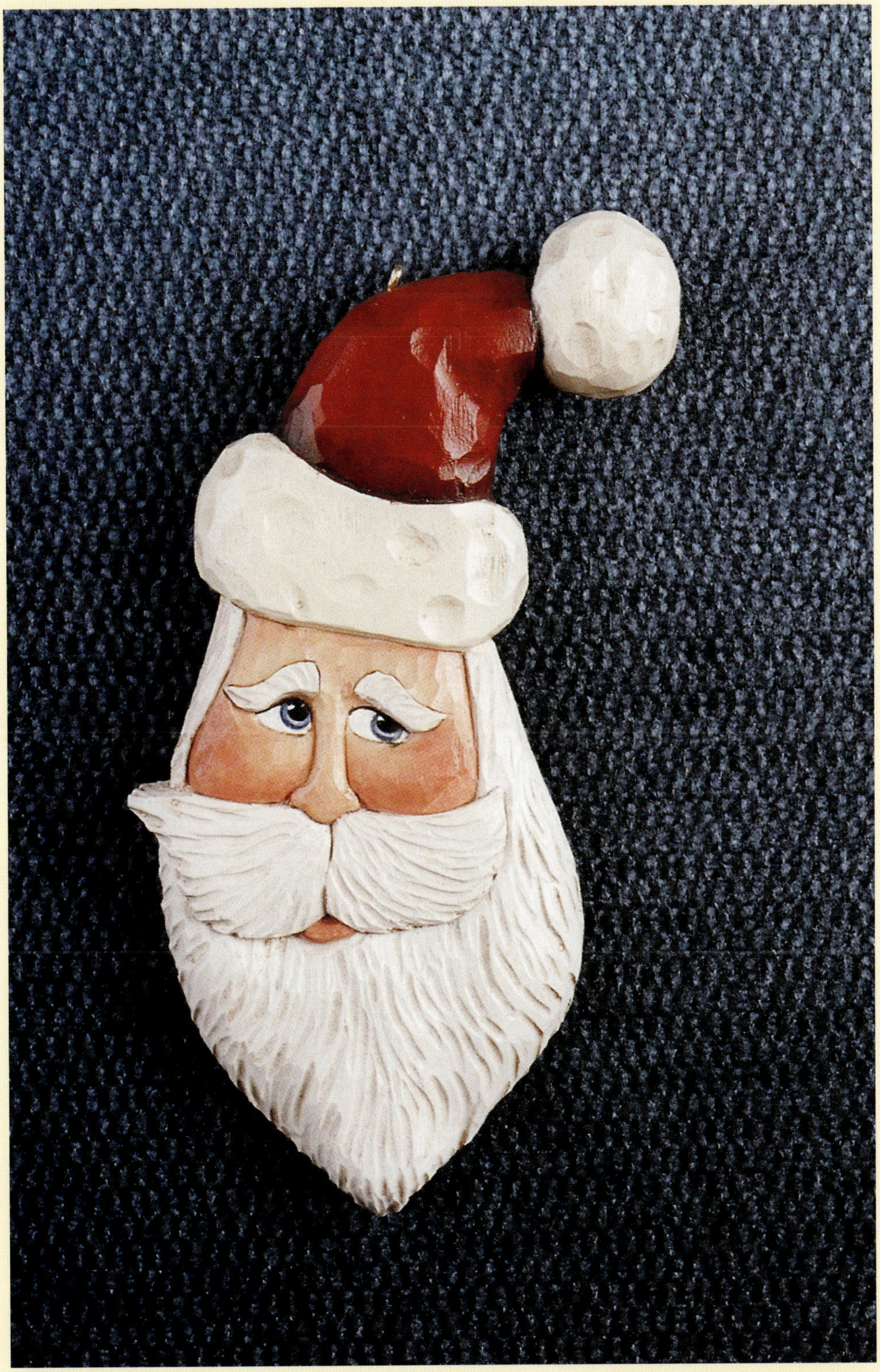

RIGHT THIS WAY SANTA

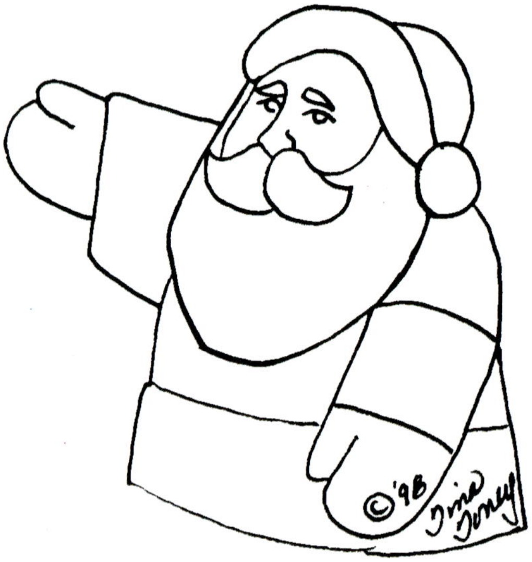

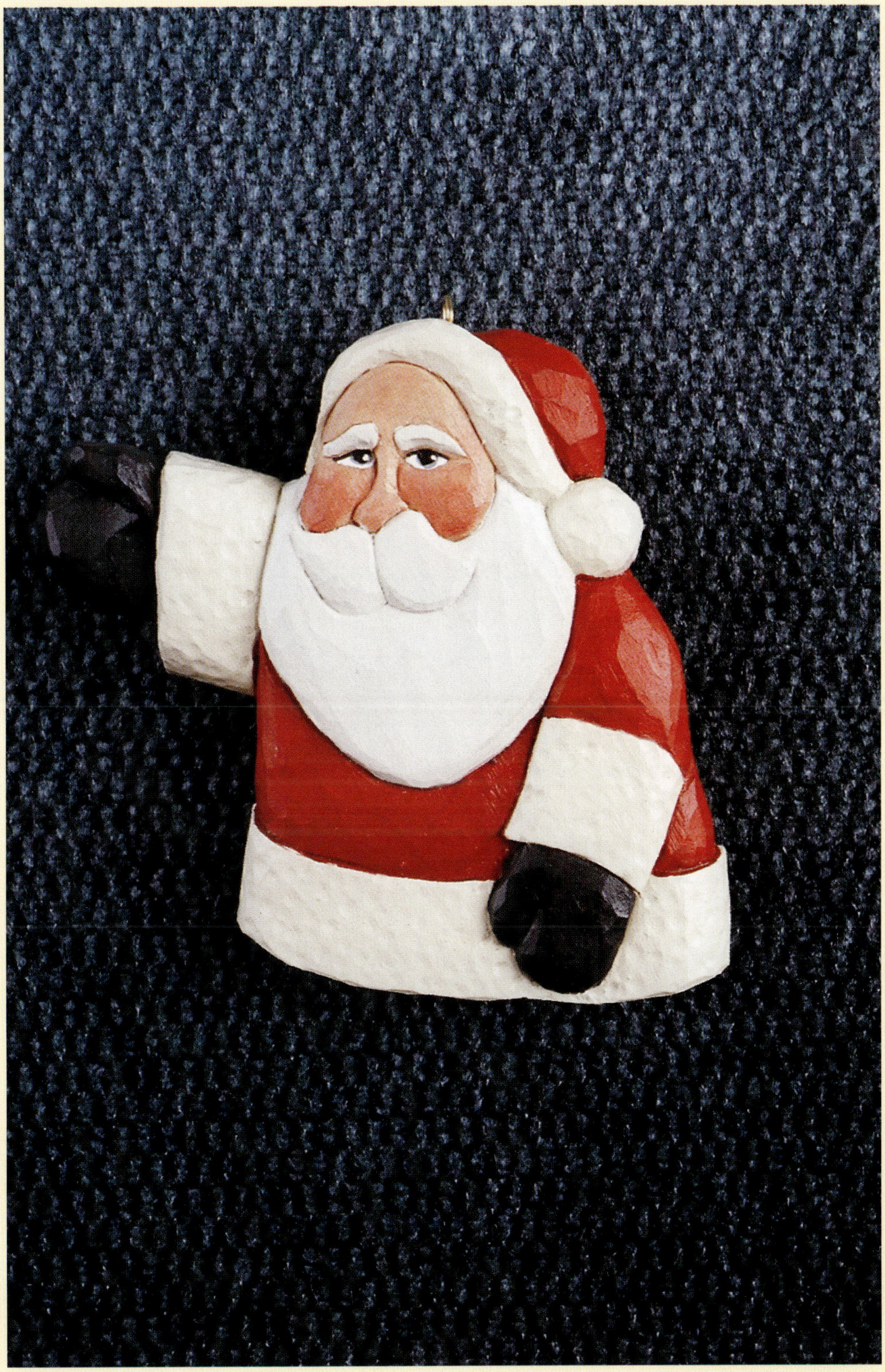

I Believe Santa

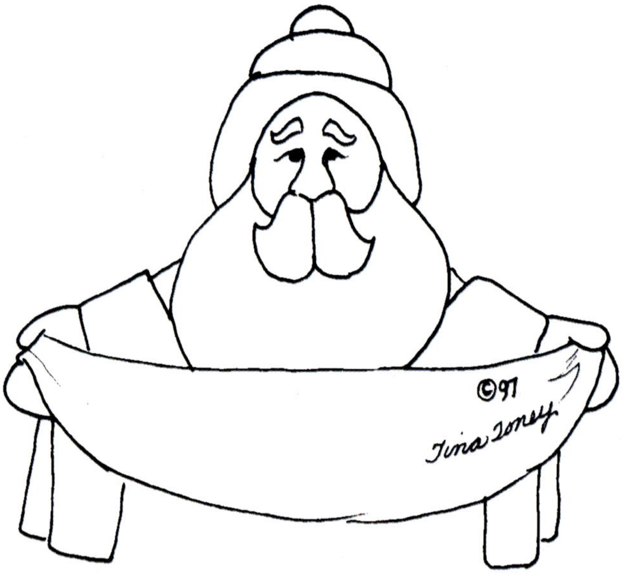

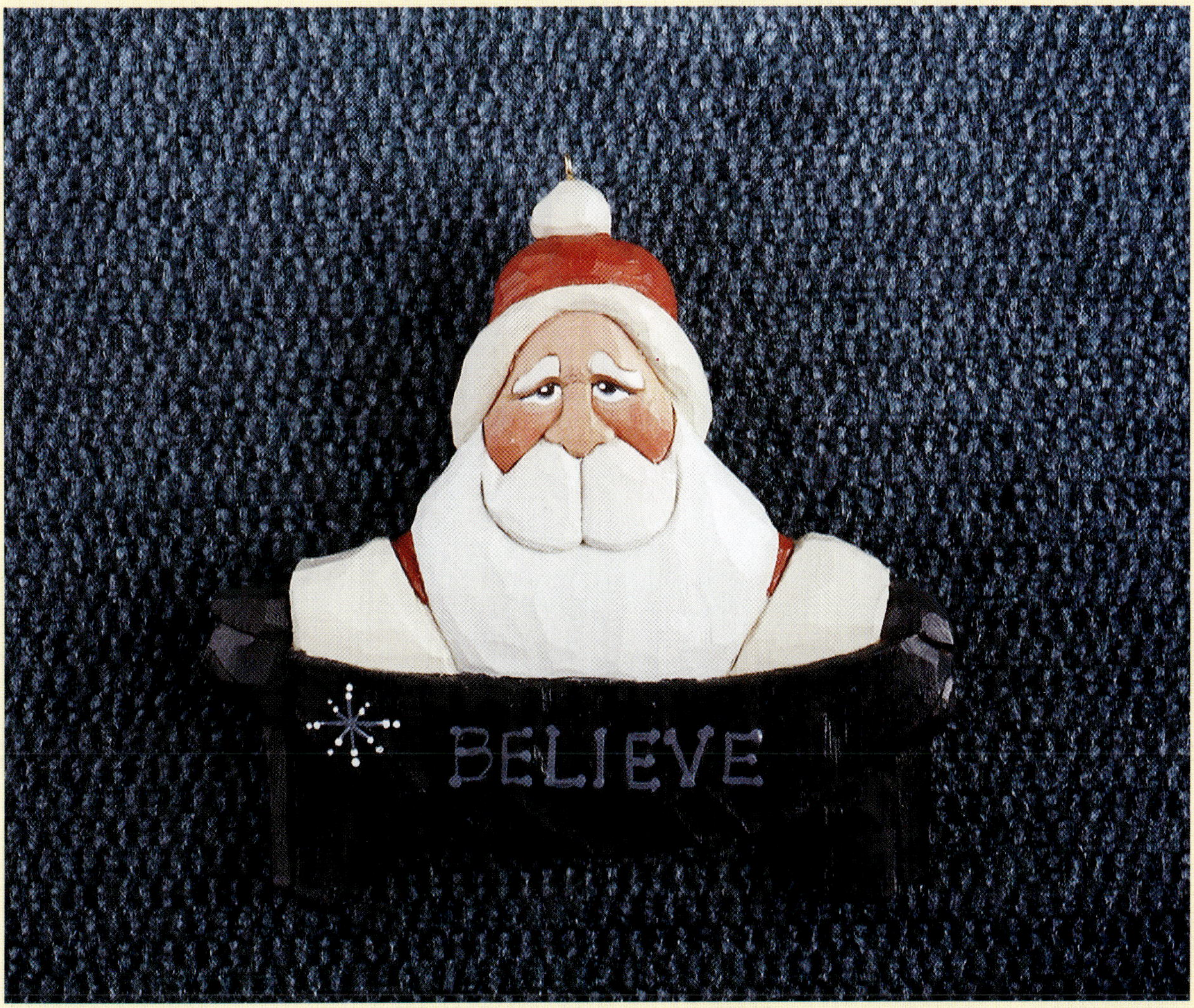
BELIEVE

More Books by the Experts

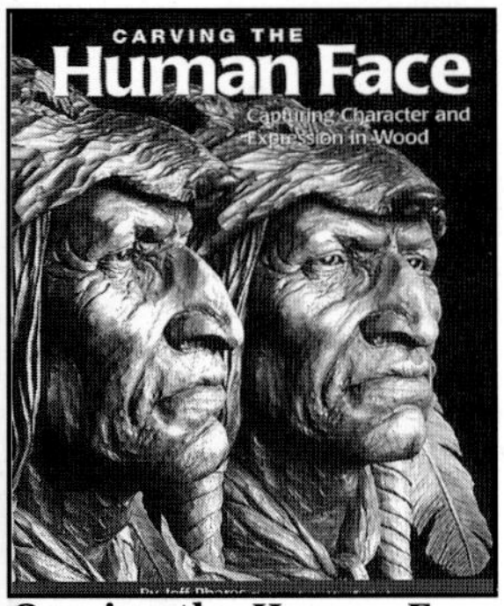

Carving the Human Face
By Jeff Phares
The best book available on carving faces! A full color guide is included.
104 pages, 8.5x11", soft cover.
$24.95 • 1-56523-102-3

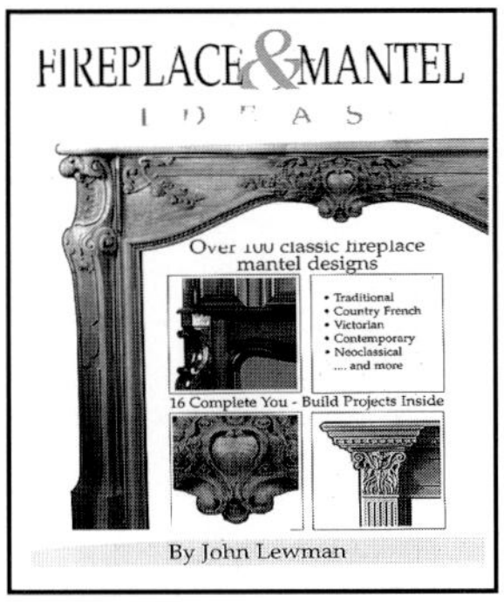

Fireplace & Mantel Ideas
By John Lewman
15 ready-to-use patterns and hundreds of photos showing installation and design.
90 pages, 8.5x11, soft cover.
$19.95 • 1-56523-106-6

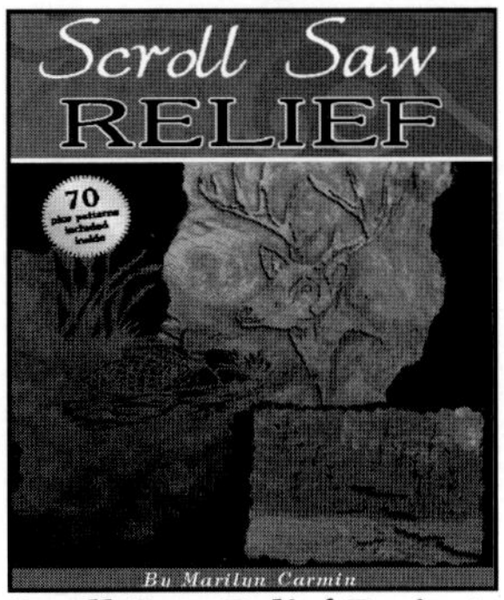

Scroll Saw Relief Projects
By Marilyn Carmin
The first book on fret and relief work. Includes more than 100 patterns.
120 pages, 8.5x11, soft cover.
$14.95 • 1-56523-107-4

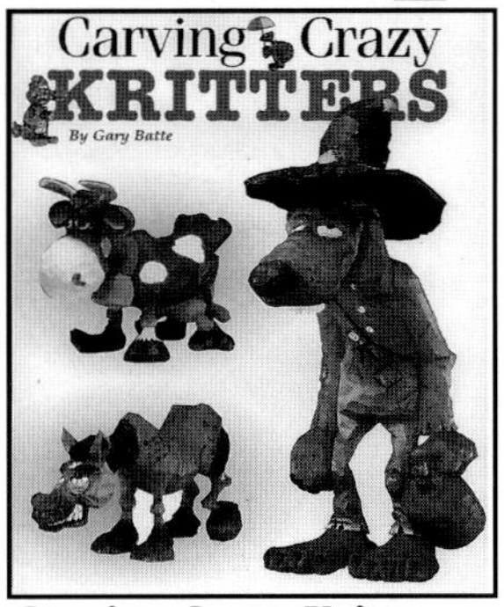

Carving Crazy Kritters
By Gary Batte
Full of creative new designs for caricature animals. A real winner!
64 pages, 8.5x11, soft cover.
$14.95 • 1-56523-114-7

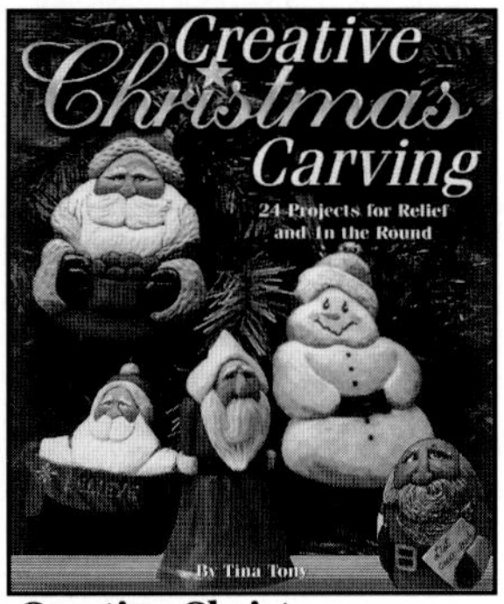

Creative Christmas Carvings
By Tina Toney
A beautiful and practical full-color guide to exciting holiday carving projects.
64 pages, 8.5x11, soft cover.
$14.95 • 1-56523-120-1

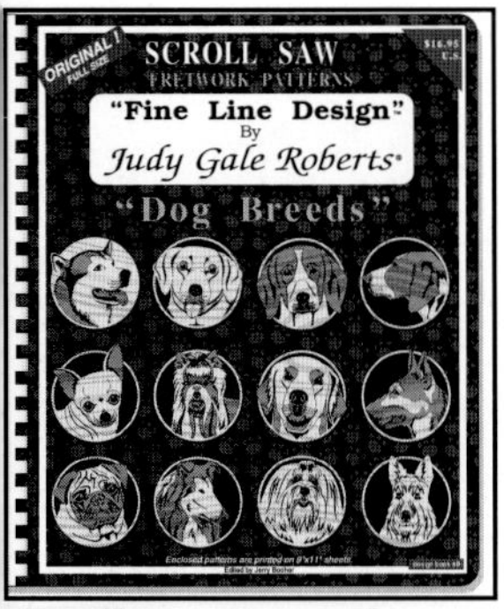

Scroll Saw Fretwork Patterns ~ Dog Breeds
By Judy Gale Roberts
Includes dozens of all-new designs of "man's best friend".
60 pages, 8.5x11, soft cover-spiral bound.
$16.95 • 1-883083-08-7

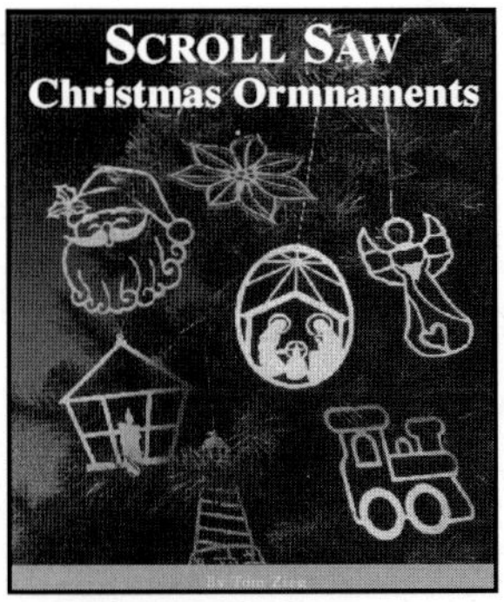

Scroll Saw Christmas Ornaments
By Tom Zieg
Over 200 ornament patterns, with brass, copper and plastic designs.
64 pages, 8.5x11, soft cover.
$9.95 • 1-56523-123-6

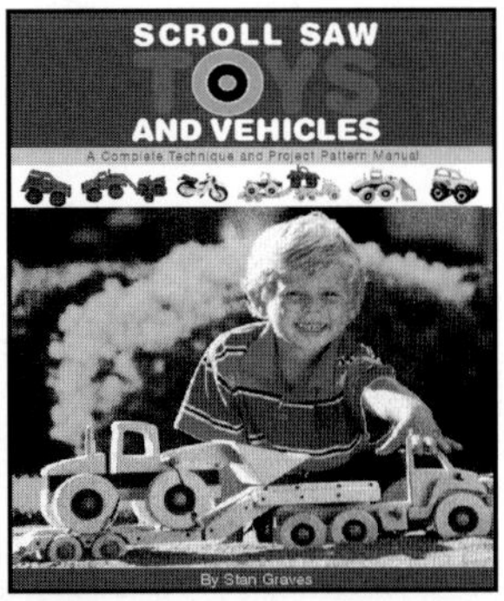

Scroll Saw Toys and Vehicles Technique & Pattern Manual
By Stan Graves
Create easy, fun toys on your scroll saw with everyday materials.
56 pages, 8.5x11, soft cover.
$12.95 • 1-56523-115-5

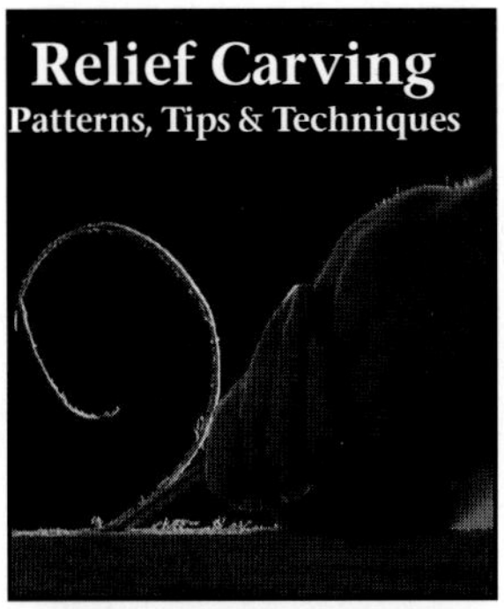

Relief Carving ~ Patterns, Tips & Techniques
By William F. Judt
A complete introduction to relief carving. Learn tricks of the trade!
120 pages, 8.5x11, soft cover.
$19.95 • 1-56523-124-4

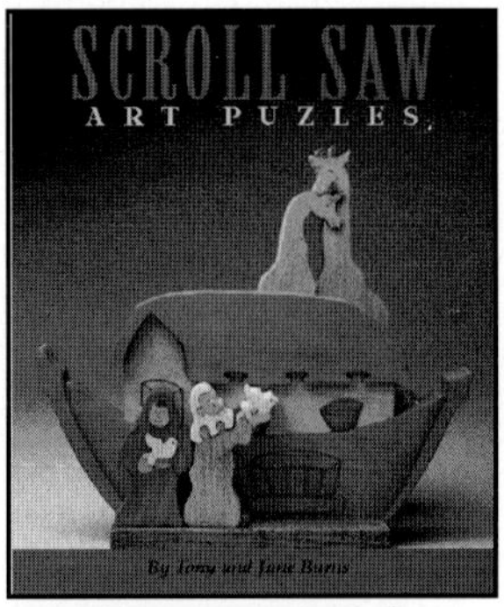

Scroll Saw Art Puzzles
By Tony and June Burns
Includes 32 patterns for cute, classical and whimsical puzzles.
80 pages, 8.5x11, soft cover.
$14.95 • 1-56523-116-3

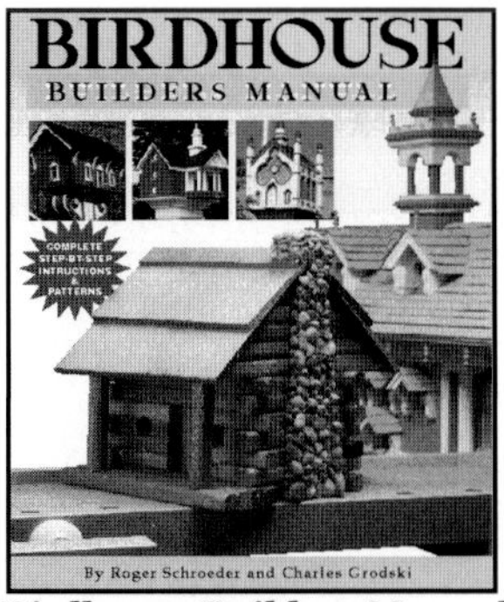

Birdhouse Builders Manual
By Roger Schroeder and Charles Grodshi
Full patterns, step-by-step photos and instructions. Sure to please!
120 pages, 8.5x11, soft cover.
$19.95 • 1-56523-100-7

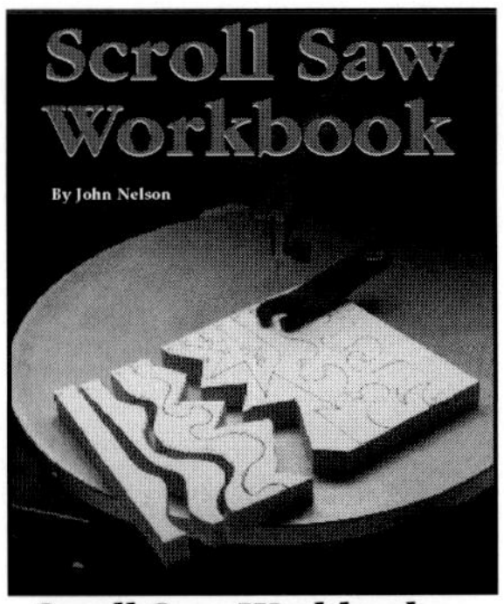

Scroll Saw Workbook
By John Nelson
The best beginner's technique book from noted author John Nelson.
96 pages, 8.5x11, soft cover.
$14.95 • 1-56523-117-1

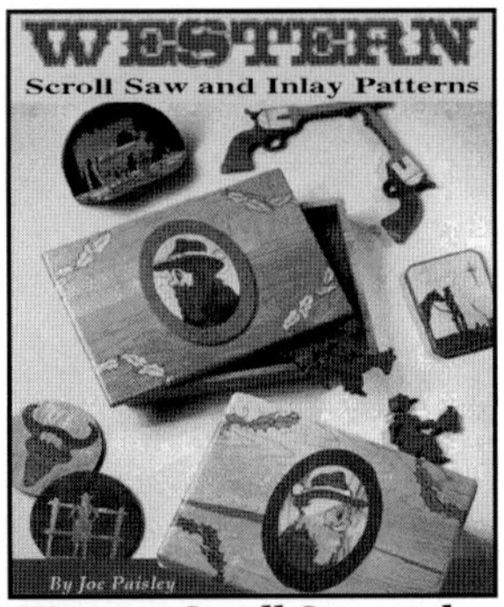

Western Scroll Saw and Inlay Patterns
By Joe Paisley
Exciting new inlay techniques and lots of new western patterns.
100 pages, 8.5x11, soft cover.
$14.95 • 1-56523-118-X

Stunning coffee table book!

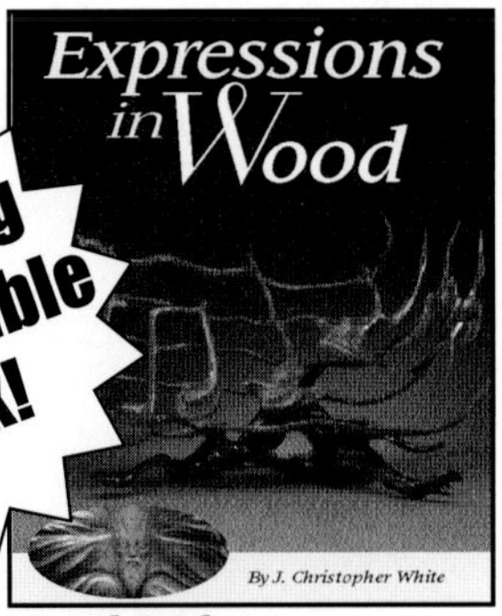

Wood Sculptures ~ Expressions In Wood
By J. Christopher White
Stylized carved wooden sculpture at its best.
128 pages, 9x12, hard cover.
$34.95 • 1-56523-122-8

Try your local book dealer first!

Canada and Foreign orders please pay in US funds using a cashier's check or by credit card (include expiration date). Please list daytime phone number for processing questions.

Shipping & handling: $2.50 per book • $5.00 maximum over 2 books

FOX BOOKS
Fox Chapel Publishing Co Inc.

Fox Chapel Publishing Company
1970 Broad Street • East Petersburg, PA • 17520

E-mail: sales@carvingworld.com

ANIMALS

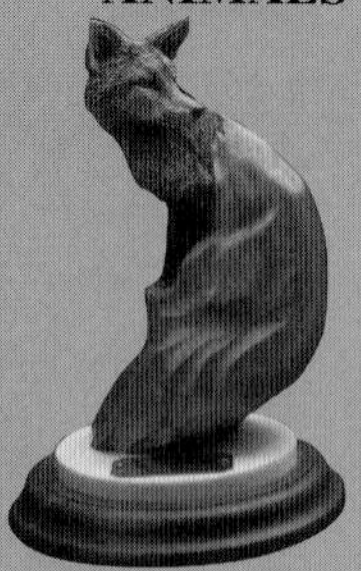

BIRDS

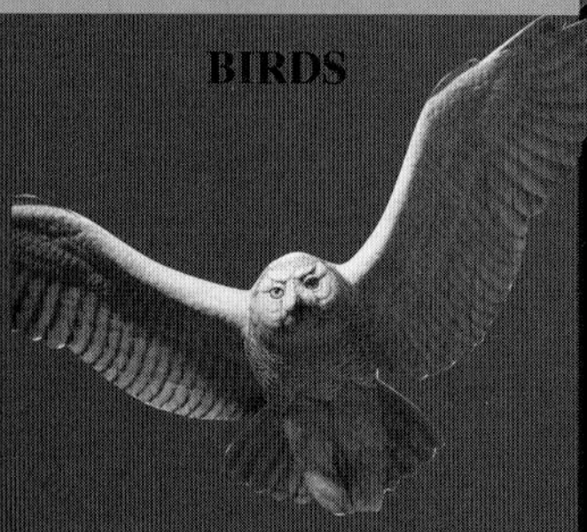

SANTAS

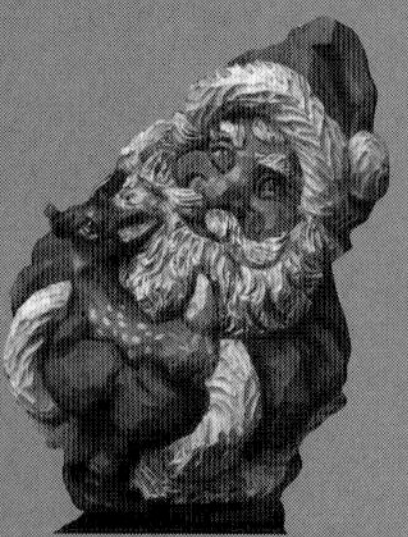

TECHNIQUES

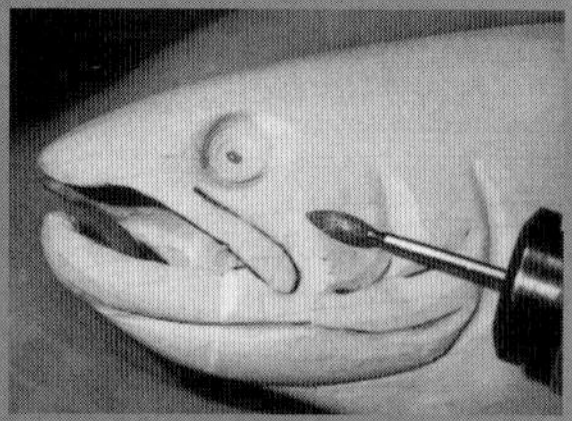

CHIP CARVING

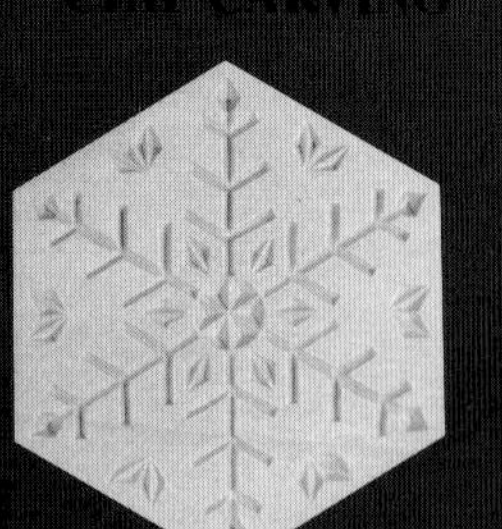

CARICATURES

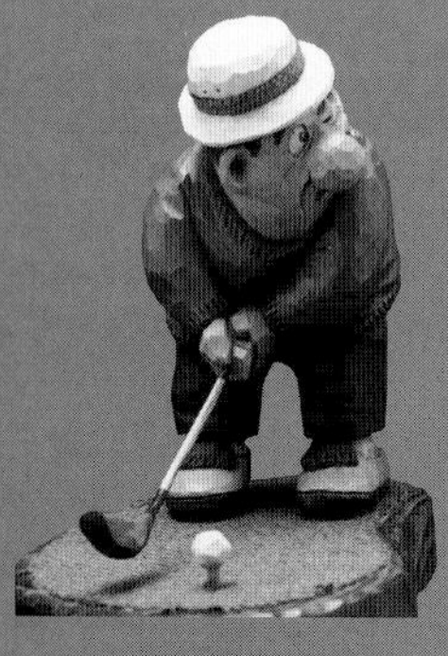

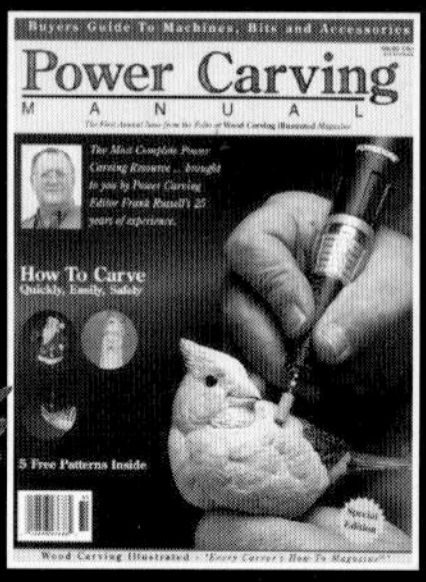

By Frank Russell

This is the definitive guide to using reciprocating and flexible shaft carving machines like the Foredom, Dremel and Ryobi. Everything you could want to know - plus patterns for 5 projects. Jam-packed issue - 120 pages in color. This is the first of our Annual series. Available now for $9.95 or FREE with a two year subscription.

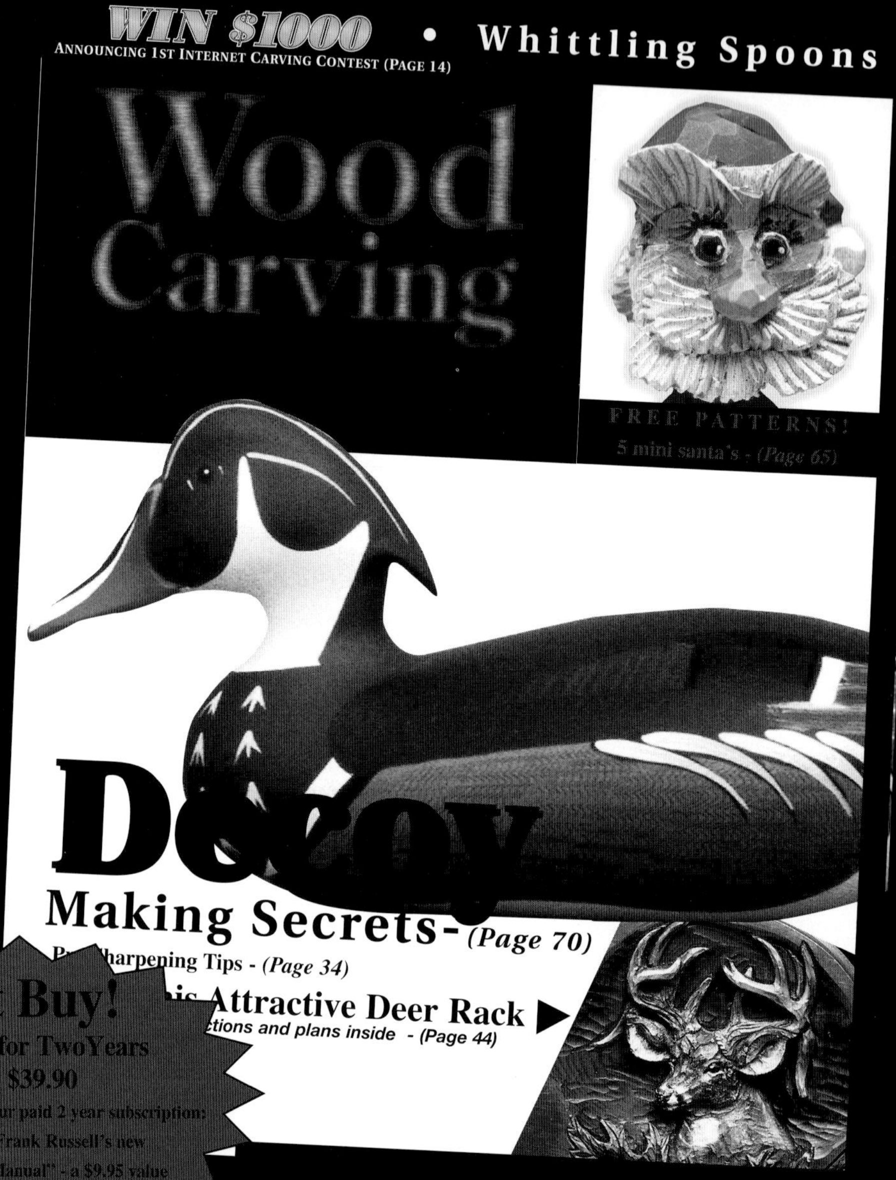

Best Buy!
Subscribe for Two Years only $39.90
Absolutely free with your paid 2 year subscription: FREE copy of Frank Russell's new "Power Carving Manual" - a $9.95 value

❑ **YES!** Please sign me up as a subscriber to **Wood Carving Illustrated**.

Money Back Guarantee If at any time you are unhappy with our magazine, write and receive a refund on any unmailed issues.

_____One Year $19.95
(Save $3.80 off the news stand price)
Canada - $22.50 Foreign - $27.95

____Two Year Special Offer $39.90
(Save $7.60 off the news stand price)
Includes the free Power Carving Annual
Canada $45.00 Foreign $55.90

(Canadian and Foreign orders please pay by money order in US Funds or by credit card)

Please allow 4-6 weeks to receive your first issue.

VISA MasterCard DISCOVER NOVUS
Sorry, no American Express.

Payment:
❑ Check ❑ Money Order ❑ Credit Card Card # ______________ Expiry:________

Please mail with payment to:
Wood Carving Illustrated Magazine
1970 Broad Street, Suite 301
East Petersburg, PA 17520

Name: ______________
Address: ______________
City: ______________ State: ________ Zip: ______________
Country: ______________

Credit Card Orders can order Toll Free **1-888-506-6630** or Fax to 717-560-4702.
Subscription Order Desk open from 9 am - 5 pm Eastern Time, Monday - Friday.